S. Scott

D1150663

Reproduced by courtesy of the London Borough of Tower Hamlets Amenities Committee

W. W. Jameson

BOROUGH ENGINEER.

JUNE 1902.

BETWEEN HIGH WALLS

BETWEEN HIGH WALLS

A London Childhood
by
GRACE FOAKES

with an Introduction by
LADY HENRIQUES, C.B.E.

and drawings by
DINAH DRYHURST

PERGAMON PRESS
Headington Hill Hall
Oxford OX3 0BW

First published 1972 by
Shepheard-Walwyn (Publishers) Ltd.
56 Doughty Street, London W.C.1
© Grace Foakes and Shepheard-Walwyn 1972
All Rights Reserved

First published 1974
Reprinted 1976

ISBN 0 08 017979 7

Printed and bound in Great Britain by
A. Wheaton & Co., Exeter

Introduction

THIS BOOK is indeed an historical gem, which glows with a different aspect of deeply moving truth from every one of its small and finely cut facets.

That it is the work of a woman who has chosen to give an honest account of her life, not withholding any blemishes in those whom she loved, or exaggerating her own virtues, nor asking for compassion by sentimentalising her woes, makes this slender volume something much more than a tale; it is a revelation and a salutary lesson in heroism. Written in an uninhibited style, her statements grip the reader by their very simplicity, making us share her hard, yet happy life, and introducing a great many to a way of life and living conditions that they can scarcely credit to have existed.

Her descriptions of the locality, much of which was destroyed during the 1939–45 war, are faithfully penned, for its grim brickwork cast its shadows over her conciousness just as it limited her visual horizons; but where the sun penetrated she saw beauty. We learn of social problems from the sufferer's angle, even as we are honoured by being allowed to share in the glorious happiness of the family's Christmas dinner.

Personally, I am so moved by this book because I have worked and lived in the area of Stepney, which includes Wapping, Shadwell and St. George-in-the-East, for the greater part of my life, and know that the living conditions described are not exaggerated. Neither is the poverty.

We are shown how an upright way of life was possible in spite of the constant battle to keep body and soul alive; and how, despite the fact that the family were not "Church-goers" (as distinct from sending the children to Sunday school), the ethical and spiritual sides of life were successfully inculcated into the children by their parents.

That Mrs Foakes should have given to the world of today this chronicle of her life in an era beyond the ken of the rising generation, is a most fortunate event, whilst to the few of the older generation like myself who still survive, it brings back memories that are full of admiration for those thousands of men and women who had to rear their families without any "mod. cons"—and made so good a job of it.

Stepney, July 1972   *Rose Henriques*

Prologue

IF YOU HAD BEEN a visitor to London when I was a child, Tower Bridge would have been one of the first places of interest you would have gone to see. It was a beautiful bridge, spanning the Thames. From the north side you could look across and see the Tower of London. If you looked over the side of the bridge, you saw all kinds of river craft. There were tugs, barges, police boats, and large ocean-going ships. When an extra large vessel, too tall to pass underneath, needed to pass further up river the bridge would be opened. A bell was rung and all traffic was stopped at either end. The bridge would open up from the centre until it stood upright, with half on each side. The ship could then pass through and proceed to whatever wharf or warehouse it was destined for. The halves of the bridge were then lowered and the traffic allowed to resume its journeyings.

You would have seen large docks, wharves and warehouses, where ships from far away places were berthed. Great cranes would load and unload cargo of every kind. Here men would earn their living. It was a magnificent sight, and visitors would stand and gaze at the busy scene and think how wonderful it all was.

But I want to take you for another visit to show you what lay on the other side of these wharves and warehouses.

As you approached Tower Bridge from the City side you came to some stone steps, which led down to the entrance to the warehouses and to St. Katherine's Way. This was a narrow road with high walls on either side. At intervals, between each warehouse, there was a short dark passage, just wide enough for a man to walk through, leading to the river. These were known as "Shoreways". Walls! Nothing but high walls until you came to St. Katherine's Bridge, a dock bridge, which at times would open to let shipping pass from the Thames into London Docks. On you walked with the high brick walls on either side. They must have been more than sixty feet high. If you wanted to see the sky you had to stand and look straight up—you were closed in on every side—and if you were a small child it could be very frightening should you chance to walk there at night.

Walking on still further you came to another dock bridge, Hermitage Bridge. It did not open, but formed part of the dock basin. On crossing this bridge the scene changed. Now there were warehouses on one side only, the river side. Opposite them was a large block of tenement flats, which boasted the name "Royal Jubilee Buildings". I believe they were built during the Royal Jubilee Year of Queen Victoria. Nothing less royal you ever saw! Iron railings enclosed them at the front and a great cobblestone yard lay stretched behind its whole length. The tenants used it for drying washing. Behind and around these tenement buildings were narrow, mean little streets and alleyways, with small drab houses, mostly with underground kitchens, where people lived in semi-darkness for most of their lives. Three or four families occupied one house, sharing the kitchen with its one cold water tap. Sometimes the tap was in the yard outside.

This was not the world as it is today. Hot water systems were unheard of, lighting was by gas or paraffin lamps and there was no electricity. Yet the people who lived there took great pride in their homes. They were mostly dockers with large families and small incomes. This was a little community which lived almost entirely within itself. You knew everyone else and everyone else knew you.

In these surroundings I spent my childhood. I can see it all so clearly in my mind that I feel compelled to write down as many things as I can remember. There must be many older people who will recall those days and places. As I grow older I shall forget, as older people do, but I shall open my book and it will all come to life again.

CHAPTER ONE

Wapping

WE LIVED in Wapping High Street. Now "High Street" today usually means a street where there are shops of all kinds, but our High Street had very few shops. It stretched from one end of Wapping to the other, with the dock bridges in between. On each side were wharves and warehouses. The roads were made of cobblestones, with a narrow path on one side only. All traffic was pulled by horses for there were no motor cars. The drivers of these horses had great whips, with which they beat them to encourage them to pull faster. Sometimes two horses would be harnessed to one cart if the load was heavy. In winter the roads would be in a very slippery state and sometimes the poor creatures would stumble and fall. Then the driver would dismount and whip them until they struggled to their feet again. This was very cruel, for in most cases the load was far too heavy. My sister and I would watch while this went on. It was an everyday sight and nobody seemed to care, but we would hold hands and cry in sympathy for the poor creatures.

In these days of clean air and smokeless fuel, it is hard to imagine what a London fog was like sixty years ago. Everyone had a coal fire, factories sent out great clouds of sooty grime, ships and tugs were driven by steam, their funnels belching out great quantities of thick black smoke. Winter would bring to the river such fogs as you do not see today. The air was so thick and yellow that you could not see where you were going. To avoid losing yourself, you had to run your hand along the walls as you walked.

They made everything dirty. Big black pieces of soot would settle everywhere. All day the ships would send out their mournful fog warning, for it was very dangerous on the river when a fog descended. Shipping was at an almost total standstill and those boats which continued on their way were in constant danger of collision. Many men fell overboard during these fogs and, since it was impossible to find them in these conditions, they were drowned. These fogs could last for many days. They were "killer fogs" (we called them "pea-soupers") and sometimes those who had a weak chest found it impossible to breathe. Many elderly people and young babies died as a result of being out in one of these fogs.

3

Great was our relief when the sun eventually shone, dispersing the gloom, and bringing things back to normal again.

✳ ✳ ✳ ✳ ✳

CHAPTER TWO

Where I Spent my Childhood

WHEN I WAS a little girl I lived with my parents, my three brothers and my sister in one of the tenement flats in Royal Jubilee Buildings. It consisted of two bedrooms and a kitchen. My parents occupied one bedroom, and we five children shared the other. Mother divided the room with a large clothes-horse covered with a sheet, to separate boys from girls. All the available space was taken up by three beds and my father's large toolchest. The walls were distempered in a dull brown colour. What a dark and cheerless room it was.

My parents' bedroom contained a double bed, a chest of drawers, a table and a chair, two boxes placed one on top of the other, and a small marble wash-stand. There was also a sewing machine. The kitchen, which served as the main room, had four Windsor chairs, my father's chair, two stools, and a kitchen table with two leaves which we opened or shut as required. At one end of the room was a small window, in front of which stood a large clothes-wringer with wooden rollers. This shut out much of the light and took up nearly all the space at that end of the room. In one corner was a black tin sink, six inches deep, and over it a cold water tap. Next to this was a black iron gas cooker, and then the fireplace. This was an open affair with a flat top which was open at the back to allow the smoke to go up. An oven was attached to the side of the grate—it heated when you lit the fire. There was no control on this; you simply guessed the heat and cooked accordingly.

It was surprising what could be cooked in this oven, once you got the hang of it. My mother had a baking tin, which had a division in the centre. In one side she would put potatoes for baking, in the other Yorkshire pudding. Then she would put a meat stand in and on top of this went the joint. The meat, the potatoes and the Yorkshire pudding all cooked together, and the tin was turned round every now and then so that each side had a chance to be next to the hot dividing wall between the fire and the oven. Into an iron saucepan on top of the open fire would go whatever vegetable was to be cooked. When it boiled it was drawn back just enough to keep it simmering. A large iron kettle was always heating on the other side of the fire, so that there was hot water whenever it was required. These cooking utensils would get very dirty and sooty, and sometimes it if was windy or the chimney wanted sweeping smoke would blow down, giving everything a smokey taste. The ashes and cinders from the fire would fall into the hearth below, and would make such a mess on everything. It was continually being cleaned up. My mother had an iron contraption which she called "the Tidy". She placed it on the hearth in front of the fire in an effort to trap the ashes as they fell, for the hearth was cleaned each morning with hearth-stone to make it look white. On the hearth stood a steel fender which too was cleaned each day, with emery paper. This all looked very nice until you lit the fire. The fire was nice too, but not so the mess. There was dust everywhere.

On the other side of the hearth and about two feet from the floor was the cupboard in which everything had to be kept, since there was no storage space anywhere else. Underneath the cupboard and hidden from view by a small curtain were all the boots, and the cat box.

This then was the kitchen where seven people ate, played and worked. But it was warm and it was home. It was the place where my mother could always be found—and that was all that mattered.

CHAPTER THREE

My Father

I FOUND MY FATHER a very hard man to understand when I was young. He was very short and thin and had large blue eyes. I could have loved him as I did my mother, but he seemed to hold us off so that we could not approach him or sit on his knee as children love to do. I believe he had a hard life as a child, and I know that he left school at the age of ten and started work. This may have had something to do with it, but I can only surmise. In later life I came to love him very much, but at the time I speak of he was an unsociable man, unfriendly even towards the people closest to him. My mother could never have a neighbour in for a cup of tea or a chat, and we could not ask our friends in either. He did not drink or smoke and had no kind of hobby. I never knew him to have a close friend as the other men did.

Everything he did had to be precise. If he chopped the sticks for the fire, each stick would be the same length and thickness as all the others, and they would all be stacked on a ledge with not one out of place. The floor was covered with mock lino (we had no carpets) and if a portion wore out he would carefully cut it away and measure for another piece to be fitted in. Always it fitted perfectly. His motto was "If a thing is worth doing, it is worth doing well". He would not borrow or lend nor allow my mother to do so. In our household his word was law and no-body dared dispute it.

He worked hard when in a job and saw to it that we children learned the meaning of work. My mother did not have much pleasure but I do not remember her ever complaining—except on Sunday afternoons when Father would undress and get into bed, leaving her to mend his working clothes while he had his rest. This she resented very much, for the clothes were dirty from the work he had been doing and she hated handling anything that was not clean.

We had a sewing machine of the treadle type which my father decided I must learn to use. He would make me sit at that machine and, after showing me how to thread the boat-shaped bobbin and to fix the top cotton, he would stand over me and I would have to practise on it. If the wheel went backwards instead of forwards the cotton would break, so he gave me lessons on starting it so that the wheel always moved the right way. When I had mastered this he would then give me an old piece of material and would stand and watch while I practised doing "straight lines". This I simply could not do while he watched me, but he would not let me give up. Eventually I mastered this too and was able to machine perfectly. I have never forgotten those lessons or his rare smile of pleasure when he told me "I knew you could do it." I still have an old treadle machine and would not part with it for all the modern ones. Each time I use it, the words still come to my mind "I knew you could do it."

I do not know how old I was when this little event happened but I recall it clearly. We woke up one morning and Father told me to go and call a neighbour who lived several streets away. I was to say she was wanted quickly as Mother was not well. She came about an hour afterwards. Then suddenly we children heard a baby's cry and we knew we had another brother or sister. When she left a little later the neighbour told my father she would not come again as Gracie was now becoming a big girl and could carry on without her. In those days you had no midwife. Neighbours looked after each other. The doctor usually came only at the time of the delivery as each visit had to be paid for and people just could not afford more than one. Therefore the arrangement was made with whoever you were most friendly with.

This particular time was unfortunate for me. I remember it was a Sunday and we were sent to Sunday School as usual. On arriving home I found Father had heated the copper and had the tin bath arranged on two chairs, just at the right height to fit my small figure. On the floor was a great pile of washing which I had to deal with, and he wanted each piece to be clean. He fitted a large apron around me, put the water from the copper into the bath and told me to start. There were sheets, pillowcases, shirts, towels and all the rest of the family wash, including all the soiled things which had been used when the baby arrived. He showed me how to do it. First each article had to be soaped, then rolled and left to soak while the next article received the same treatment. When all were soaped and soaked then came the rubbing. A washing-board was put into the bath and I had to rub each piece on the board until it was spotless. As I finished each one my father took a look at it to see whether it was clean or not. If it was not, he gave it back to me and I had to do it again. Then he put the whites into the copper and boiled them. When all the soaping and rubbing was finished then came the rinsing. The bath was emptied into the sink and filled with clean cold water. My father fed the rinsed washing between the wooden rollers of the wringer while I turned its large handle. You who have washing machines and modern gadgets can have no idea of the tiredness and sore fingers which I had on that occasion, when it was all finished. Father rewarded my efforts by telling me he would give me a good hiding if I told what he had made me do. I need not tell you that fear of the hiding kept me quiet, and not until now have I told this story. But I have never forgotten it either!

When I was quite small my father often did nightwork at the wharf where he worked. Two ships came from Scotland, and were known as "Leith Boats". One was named "The Royal Scot", the other "The

7

Royal Fusilier". If one ship berthed alongside the wharf the other was anchored out in the river. At such a time the men would have to work all day and all night so that the one could sail and the other come alongside at the next high-water. Nobody refused to work all night, for the men were glad of the extra money. And besides, there were always men willing to take the place of any man who did refuse such long hours. Sometimes Father would come home after working all day, saying he must work all night. This he would do, returning home for breakfast in the morning. There was no day off next day. He would go back and work until tea-time. Imagine it: two days and one night without stopping. No wonder he was grumpy; he must have been tired out. But I loved the time when my father worked this way, for I went to sleep in my mother's bed. There was nothing I loved more than lying with my arms around her. I'm afraid I had little sympathy for my father's tiredness, not realising then what it must have meant to work such hours.

Father came to know the cooks aboard these ships (which carried passengers as well as cargo) and when they berthed he would buy a large enamel bowl of dripping from them. He would bring it home and send me all around the tenements and surrounding streets asking if anyone wanted any. I was given a great many basins to bring home. Father first weighed the basin then put into it a half-pound of dripping. I had to return these basins one at a time so that I did not get them muddled up. For each half-pound I received twopence. Nobody had more than half a pound as this was as much as they could afford. If they had no money then they couldn't have the dripping, for my father would not allow credit. This took me a long time and meant a lot of running up and down the tenement stairs. The profit he made paid for our own dripping. We had the best of it, for there was always lovely gravy at the bottom of the bowl. I thought it well worth the trouble of coming and going, for nothing tasted as good as that gravy spread on our morning toast. Besides, it was free—and that made it all the nicer!

CHAPTER FOUR

My Mother

MY MOTHER was a dear gentle person, who loved us all. This even made up for the lack of love from my father. She was small and, to my childish mind, quite beautiful. Her hair was white. I do not remember her ever having hair any other colour. This may have been due to ill-health for she was never very strong. Each year she would have a new baby. This was always a great surprise to us. We would wake up one morning and my father would say "You have a new brother" or "You have another sister", as the case might be. I think she had fourteen children altogether, but I am not quite sure of this, for some died at birth and some lived only a few weeks. Five of us survived and I will tell you our names in order of ages. First was Robert, then me, and then came Kathleen, William and Sydney.

We had no bathroom, so each Friday evening after tea, the tin bath, about two feet long and eighteen inches wide was brought into the kitchen and put on the floor in front of the fire. Then we would take turns to have our weekly bath, our knees tucked under our chins so that we fitted in. I always saw to it that I went in first as the water was clean and hot. After each child came out a kettle of hot water was added to warm it up for the next. At last all five of us had been bathed. I loved my bath, for a hot towel would be hanging on the fire guard to dry me with.

We were never normally allowed to lie in bed, not even on Sunday. Only when we were feeling unwell was it permitted. I loved the times when I was poorly, because Mother would come and give me hot bread and milk sprinkled with sugar. It never failed to make me feel better. I think the extra bit of loving helped me as much as the bread and milk.

CHAPTER FIVE

Haircuts and Brass Buttons

IT WAS an unheard of thing, when I was young, to cut a girl's hair. Only girls with dirty heads had their hair cut. Every so often, a nurse visited the school and if a girl was found to have vermin, or traces of them, she was sent to the cleansing station. (I do not know where this was, but we lived in great fear of going there.) The child's hair was cropped close to her head, and she was given a disinfectant hair wash. This was considered a great disgrace and she would be shunned by the other girls. It was hardly surprising then that every day, without fail, my mother would undo our plaits, and comb through our hair with a small-tooth comb. If we so much as scratched our heads, she would stop whatever she was doing and look to see if we had picked up anything. Each Friday night at bath time she would wash our heads with soda water and Sunlight soap, and then plait it into many plaits. These would not be undone until Sunday, when they were loosed, crimped and shining.

My brothers went to a Jewish barber who lived about half-an-hour's walk away, in Cable Street. He would give them what was called a "prison crop". Every bit of hair was shaved off. Needless to say, this was very cold in winter, but the hair took longer to grow if cut this way and that meant it would be a long time before another haircut was needed. For this a charge of twopence was made, and at the end of the ordeal each boy received a little gift, to encourage him to go again. My brother William, having very fair hair, used to look bald when he had his hair cut this way, and much to his disgust the other children used to call him Claudie Whitehead. He was known by this name for a long time.

One day when William was quite a small boy, Kathleen and I took him to a little park not far from Royal Jubilee Buildings. Now it was the fashion at that time for little boys to wear brass buttons on their over-coats, which were double-breasted and called "reefer coats". William had six shining buttons on his coat, and my mother was very proud of them. We played for a long time. When it became warm we took William's coat off and laid it on a seat, forgetting all about it. We saw other children playing near the seat, but did not attach any importance to this. Imagine our dismay when, picking up the coat before going home, we found all the buttons had been cut off. It was a long time before we dared to go home, because we were afraid Father would find out. However, we managed to get the coat hung up on its peg, and we said nothing until Mother was alone. We knew she would be cross, but this we did not mind. I'm glad to say she quietly sat and sewed six black buttons on the coat. Father never noticed that the brass ones had gone. But never again did William have shining brass buttons.

Kathleen and I loved that little park. Each Saturday morning in summer we would try and go there. Our greatest delight was to take off our boots and stockings. We stuffed our stockings into our boots, which we hung around our necks by their laces so that we would not lose them. We would spend all morning running and dancing about in bare feet, making them very dirty. The feeling of bare feet on warm asphalt is something I shall always remember; somehow there was a freedom in skipping around barefoot. My mother would wonder how we managed to get our feet so dirty on Saturdays, but of course we never told.

Some days, before starting off for school, Kathleen and I would ask Mother if we could have a farthing with which to buy some sweets. Now my mother's skirts always had one very large pocket inserted into the seam, and into this pocket went all kinds of things—a thimble, pieces of string, a handkerchief and anything she wanted to hide from us children. We would stand hopefully waiting while she felt in her pocket. She would sometimes find a farthing right at the bottom. She would give it to me, with the reminder that I must share it with Kathleen.

We passed a small sweet shop on our way to school. The owner was a most obliging man. He would let us stand and choose whatever we wanted. His sweets were priced four ounces for one penny, so that with our farthing we could get one ounce. When we finally made up our minds we would ask him for whatever we fancied and request him to put it into two papers, so that we each had a fair share. He always did this and we went off to school with half an ounce each. When I see parents giving their children so much money these days I never fail to think of a farthing between two.

CHAPTER SIX

Four Meals for Fourpence

I DO NOT WANT the reader to suppose we were an unhappy family. Indeed, my childhood on the whole was a very happy one. Certainly we were poor and my father earned little money, but my mother was a wonderful housekeeper. How she did it I do not know, but we were always well fed, neat and tidy.

I remember how she would send me for twopennyworth of bones, and tell me to ask the butcher "Would you mind leaving a little meat on?" I used to come home with a great many bones, which my mother would put into a large iron saucepan. She cooked them until the meat was tender and then left the pan to cool. In the morning there was a thick layer of dripping on the top. This she would carefully remove and put into a basin, ready for our morning toast, which was all we had for breakfast. Next came the bones. These were scraped clean of all the meat, of which there was usually enough to fill a pie dish. With the aid of some of the dripping, Mother made these scrapings into a meat pie. And, my, what a pie that was! It gave seven hungry people a wonderful dinner. Before the next meal I was sent for one pennyworth of pot herbs. For the penny you could have one onion, a few carrots and some turnips. These were cooked, along with a handful of barley, in the juice in which the bones had been boiled. This made a large pan of stew which did for two days' dinner.

Perhaps you can now get some idea of what household management had to be like in my early childhood. In all, those three dinners and a breakfast cost about fourpence. My mother was not alone in her economy. The force of circumstances demanded it. Money was short and appetites were large, so women in those days were obliged to be thrifty.

* * * * *

CHAPTER SEVEN

Watney Street and more about my Mother

WATNEY STREET was a narrow street leading from Cable Street through to Commercial Road. It was half an hour's walk from home, and we did our weekly shopping there on Saturdays. There were shops on both sides of the road and stalls lined it from one end to the other. In winter the stalls would be brightly lit with naked naphtha lights, and all the stallholders stood by their wares and shouted and called as you went by, trying to get your custom. When she was well enough to go, Mother would take me with her to help carry the shopping home. Her first buy would be the Sunday joint, which was half a leg of mutton, costing 1s. 11d.—she would never pay more. She would ask the butcher to cut a slice off the top, about an inch thick. She called this a cutlet and it was cooked the following morning for our breakfast. She fried it and cut it into seven portions (one for each of us) and served it with a spoonful of fried tomatoes, which she had bought for about fourpence a pound as they were over-ripe.

She bought the vegetables next, including 12 lbs of potatoes at 4 lbs for twopence. She would buy a few halfpenny oranges (we had a half orange each, never a whole one). Then we moved on to the salt stall where a woman would stand sawing up large blocks of salt, which she sold at about 2 lbs for a halfpenny. On we walked, passing the stall where a woman was grating horseradish. Her eyes would be watering from the strong smell of it. She would sell it at one or two pennies a bag. One shop sold cooked sheep's heads. I could not bear to look at them, but they were considered a great treat. Then there were the "Rag Girls", as they were called, women with stalls full of other people's unwanted clothes. Usually they had their stalls in a side street where it was a little quieter, and there you could see groups of women examining the clothes, in search of a bargain. I once stood watching Mother while she sorted the clothes over. No article was ever more than a copper or two and on this occasion she was very pleased for she managed to buy quite a large bundle of baby clothes for fourpence. When we got home she washed them and put them away for the new baby, which I only then realised was soon due to arrive.

Soon after the visit to Watney Street during which she had bought the baby clothes, Mother was taken ill. Father called the doctor who examined her and said she must go to hospital. She went to the London Hospital in Whitechapel Road, where she was told she must have an operation for the removal of a tumour. Arrangements had to be made for all of us children to be looked after. Offers were made for each of us to stay with a different neighbour, and Mother then went into hospital. She had the tumour safely removed and stayed in hospital for about three weeks. Then she returned home to await the arrival of the new baby. On our wall we penned a motto to greet her. It said "What is a home without a Mother". Mottoes were in fashion in those days. Usually you saw them at Christmas time, but on this occasion it was our "Welcome Home" greeting to our mother.

A few weeks after this the baby was born. It was a boy and Mother named him Wilfred. We were allowed into her room to see him. I remember my mother telling me to be specially careful with him. "He hasn't come to stay", she said. "He's only lent to us for a little while." Wilfred was a poor weak baby and, on thinking about it now, I believe he had no chance of living. When he was six weeks old he was taken into Great Ormond Street Children's Hospital, and within a few days we had news that he was dead.

CHAPTER EIGHT

Green Bank

I WONDER WHO was responsible for the name of this street. When I first learned to read, these were two of the first words I remember spelling out. "Green Bank." Such a lovely name! It summoned up a picture of a cool and beautiful place, covered with grass. Here wild flowers would grow. Here one might lie in the sun on warm days and dream of fields beyond, of quiet country lanes, of birds, of butterflies. The longing for such a place was always with me. I would walk along that street and shut my eyes, willing it to be as I wanted.

Alas, it never happened. When I opened my eyes it was still there—a narrow wretched street full of tiny houses. Each had a small window in line with the front door, which gave straight on to the living room, a room so dark that even on a summer's day you could not see unless you lit a lamp. These houses faced each other across a road which was just wide enough to allow the passage of a horse and cart. On summer evenings people sat on the doorsteps chatting and gossping until the dark sent them indoors. You must remember that there was neither radio nor television then, and nothing to do when day was done but to sit in the street and gossip. I have no idea how such a street came to have such a name. I only know that it was always a disappointment to me each time I saw it.

* * * * *

CHAPTER NINE

The Month of May

I HAVE FOND MEMORIES of the month of May, because it was a month in which so many nice things happened. The first of May was "May Day". For weeks we had been learning such songs as "Now is the Month of Maying". In one verse the words include the phrase "Each with his bonnie lass is dancing on the grass", and I would think to myself "Where is the grass?" However, I loved the song, and I determined that one day I would "dance on the grass". At school a maypole was erected in the playground, and some of us danced around it. The girls who were chosen wore white dresses, and as I never had one I was never chosen. Our mothers were invited to come and listen to the singing and to watch the dancing. This was a lovely day for we were given a half-day holiday in the afternoon.

I remember that May 24th was Empire Day. We were taught all the current patriotic songs and had our hair tied with red, white and blue ribbon. Every child had a flag to wave in honour of "Our Glorious Empire", as it was called. We sang of our lands and possessions overseas. We sang of "Deeds of Glory". We sang, and believed we were the mightiest nation on earth. But how many, I wonder, felt as I did. While all this went on I'm afraid I sang with my mouth only, not from the heart. For I saw only those same high walls and thought to myself, "We sing of our possessions, while not one of us here owns as much as a flowerpotful of earth." However, a second half-day holiday followed upon the singing, and the sad thoughts of the morning were soon forgotten in the joy of planning what we should play at in the afternoon.

Another event each May was the Catholic Procession, which was held on Sunday in about the middle of the month. There were many Irish Catholic families in Wapping and each made a grotto outside their house. This usually sheltered a statue of the Virgin Mary, with the child Jesus in her arms. It was quite a sight to see one standing in the doorway, surrounded by all kinds of decorations and ornaments. All the Catholics walked through the streets, the girls dressed in white dresses and white shoes, and with a white veil covering their heads and faces. They walked very slowly, singing the virtues and praises of the Virgin Mary. The procession halted at each grotto while the priest went and knelt and blessed it and the people in the house outside which it stood. It was a moving and impressive sight and we would follow and wonder what it all meant. We enjoyed watching it, but what I could not understand (and I don't think I ever will), was that after it had all finished and the grottoes had been taken down, most of the people concerned ended the day by going to the nearest public house and getting drunk, and making merry with singing and dancing. I used to think and wonder how such a moving procession could end in such a way.

CHAPTER TEN

My Friend Winifred

WHEN I WAS not playing with my sister I would go to Winifred's. She too lived in the tenements but on the top floor, six stories up. In order to earn a little more money many women went daily to offices in the City, where they cleaned and dusted, either before the staff arrived or when they had left. Winifred's mother went office cleaning morning and evening, and every time I went to Winifred's her mother would be setting off for work. I remember how she would say "Now, Winifred, when your father comes home from work you know he won't feel well. You must be gentle with him and help him into bed." I thought this very strange until one day I saw why.

Poor man, he worked in the local brewery and drank himself drunk. Only instinct brought him home. He crawled up those six flights of stone steps and knocked at the door. Winifred warned me to keep quiet while she helped him in and coaxed him into his chair. Then, talking to him all the while as if he were a baby, she took off his clogs and socks and led him into the bedroom, where she managed to sit him on the bed and undress him. Then she laid him down on his bed to sleep until the morning. This done, we then played until it was time for me to go home. Winifred must have been about ten years old at the time. I often think of her and wonder if she remembers those days as vividly as I do.

✳ ✳ ✳ ✳ ✳

CHAPTER ELEVEN

Aunt Amy

AUNT AMY was my mother's aunt. She thought she was about eighty years old but she did not know the exact year in which she had been born, nor on what day of the month her birthday fell. It didn't seem to worry the old lady at all. She had never been to school so she could not read or write. She was a small fat little woman, with bright black eyes which were always smiling. Whenever she went out she wore a little black bonnet trimmed with jet beads, a short black cape and springside boots. She was a widow, and existed on her old age pension of 2s. 6d. a week, plus a shilling or two now and then from the Parish relief. She lived in one room, with few comforts other than a small fire grate and a gas ring. Her bed was in one corner.

I used to visit her sometimes, for I was very fond of her. She would visit us too but only when my father was out. She felt he did not welcome her—which was true. Mother would give her any cast-off clothes she had, and Aunt Amy was always most grateful to have them. Sometimes when she came, Mother would persuade her to stay to tea, telling her to take no notice of Father's moods. He did not like her because she took snuff, which he said was a dirty habit. Aunt Amy was the only relative who ever came to see us. I think Father's attitude kept the others away. (Yet Mother never found fault with him; for I think, despite all his funny ways, she loved him.)

Sometimes Aunt Amy would borrow a shilling from my mother. Mother knew that this would never be paid back but she lent it all the same. Aunt Amy would keep away for a week or two after she had been lent money. Then I would go and call on her and ask her why she hadn't been to see us. We all pretended that we had quite forgotten about the shilling and so she would come again. In due course she would borrow another shilling. A shilling would see her over the weekend, and on the following Monday she could collect her old age pension for the week. I cannot possibly see how she managed to live and pay her rent, but there were many like her in those days when I was young.

✳ ✳ ✳ ✳ ✳

CHAPTER TWELVE

The Workhouse and Father Wainwright

TODAY the word "workhouse" is little used, but during my childhood it was common enough. The workhouse was the institution into which old people were put if they had nobody to care for them. Everyone dreaded the thought of ending up there.

When old people became ill they were taken off to the infirmary and transferred to the workhouse when they were better. Everyone there was dressed in a uniform, the men in thick navy suits and the women in thick navy dresses; you always knew where they lived the moment you saw them—their clothes gave them away. I have known many an old person who struggled to exist on a few shillings a week rather than go there. I don't think they were badly treated. It was the indignity of it which was so hard to bear, and even people as poor as these had their pride. I remember my mother being very angry when she heard that a committee had met to consider how to cut down costs. This committee consisted of some of the more wealthy parishioners. One of them sugges-ted that the old men could do without underpants and the old women without drawers. I am happy to say that the rest of the committee refused to do this. Nearly everyone who heard the story completely ignored the offender, for their sympathies were very much with the old people.

If you crossed the Dock Bridge, or lived beyond it, you were said to be "on the other side". Neither the grown-ups nor the children "on the other side.' had anything to do with us. They were a community on their own and so were we, although we were all in one parish.

It was a common sight to see Sisters of Mercy coming or going on various errands. These nuns were from St. Peter's church, which was on the other side. They wore long black flowing robes and went stockingless. Their hair was shaved off and they each wore on their heads an enormous stiff white arrangement which looked like wings, so that they gave you the impression they were flying. We children called them "Flying Angels". In their spare time they sewed and made garments which they sold to the poor at a very low charge. Every year my mother would go and buy Kathleen and me a check gingham dress each, which cost her two shillings. She would bring them home and sew a piece of lace around the neck to pretty them up. Throughout the summer we wore these as our Sunday dresses and they really did look very nice.

The priest of St. Peter's was a small man named Father Wainwright. He wore a long shabby black cloak and a large flat felt hat, and always carried a big walking stick. He was very highly thought of by everybody and, although this was a very rough area and drunken fights were often breaking out, if anyone was in trouble of any sort you had only to ask Father Wainwright to call and he would come. If a child was ill, or a family bereaved he was always there to comfort or help. One day he met a homeless man and took him for a meal; then in a doorway he took off his shirt and gave it to the man. Father Wainwright lived to a great age and he was regarded as a saint by the people of Wapping. In 1967 when I revisited this place I went by his church and on a plaque on the wall I saw his name and history. I am sure there are many like me who still remember him.

CHAPTER THIRTEEN

Events I particularly Remember

THERE WERE no gardens, trees or flowers in our little community. Most of the houses had a small yard at the back, and the toilet was always in this. We grew up with the streets as our playground. I had a great longing for grass to play on.

There was a small park some distance away but we could not go on the grass because of the notices up warning us to keep off. Now, if you had grown up in conditions like these you might have had some experience of the great longing that comes to a child for the sight of trees and flowers. As I mentioned earlier, Kathleen and I would go to this little park whenever we had the chance.

On going one day I suddenly had a grand plan. I would make a window-box and fill it with lovely flowers! But where was I to get the wood? And where, if I got the wood, could I get some earth? And then, where to get the flowers? I think I must have been a very pushing sort of child because I managed all three. First the wood; I begged an orange crate from a boy who worked for a greengrocer, pulled it to pieces very carefully (for I needed all the nails), then set to work and made the window-box. You never saw a window-box like it in all your life, but to me it was wonderful. The next thing was the earth. I haunted that little park for days, until finally I plucked up enough courage to ask the park keeper if he would give me some earth.

"But what if I do?" he said. "How will you carry it home? Earth is very heavy you know." Here indeed was one thing I had not thought of.

"If I come each day after school with a bag, will you fill it for me?" I asked. He promised he would. So each day I would go with a small bag and he would fill it for me. It took a long time, but at last my window-box was full of lovely earth. Then came the biggest problem. Where were my plants to come from? I decided I would earn some money somehow, but I found that nobody wanted a small girl to do anything. Then, going to the park one day, I met my friendly park keeper.

"How's the window-box?" he asked.

Sadly I told him I could not get any plants. To my great joy he gave me some, telling me how to dig them in and look after them. I shall

23

never be able to describe what I felt when the plants were in the box. By today's standards they were poor things, but to me they appeared beautiful. No plants anywhere were ever tended so carefully or loved so much. Such were the simple pleasures of childhood, which I hope I shall never forget.

Another little story tells again of my love of flowers. I have said a little about my mother, who was never well. One year she had been worse than usual, having had a baby and lost it after a few weeks. I remember how sad she looked and I longed to make her happy. Going through the little park one day I suddenly had an idea. Here were lovely flowers. I would take a flower home to my mother. There were beds of dahlias of many colours, large and beautiful—surely they wouldn't miss one flower. I stood and watched until no one was looking. Then I hurried over the grass and picked a huge bloom. It was bright, bright red. I carried it gently in my small hands.

Suddenly a boy came around the corner. He walked up to me and asked for the flower, but I would not give it to him. He offered me two-pence for it and I would not agree to this either. It was for my mother and nobody else should have it, not even for twopence, which was quite a lot for a small girl to have. I hurried home and gave the flower to her. I cannot tell you who was the happier, she at receiving it or me at giving it, even though I had stolen it. This last bit, of course, I never told her. I said it had been given to me by my friendly park keeper.

I do not remember where I got it from, but one day I found myself the proud possessor of threepence. Mother was ailing still and had to spend the time in bed. I decided to go to the market where we did our weekly shopping and on this occasion I went by myself. I was about ten years old and a true little Cockney child. After walking for nearly an hour, I reached the market. I strolled up and down looking at the stalls, on which were displayed goods of every description. Threepence was such a lot to spend, so I wanted to choose carefully. Then I saw them: lovely peaches! But they cost sixpence each, so how was I to buy one for three-pence? I stood and looked for so long that I think the stallholder thought I was up to no good. He asked me what I wanted and I told him that I wanted a peach for my mother, but that I only had threepence. He scratched his head, looked me up and down, then said he might be able to find one which was a bit over-ripe. After thorough searching he held one out to me. Eagerly I took it and handed him my threepence. I cupped my hands together with the peach resting between them and started on my long walk home. In my mind's eye I could see the joy on my mother's face when I gave the peach to her. Then to my horror a boy came along and grabbed the peach out of my hands. Off he ran, and so did I, racing after him. I do not think I had ever run so fast before. My Cockney blood was up and I ran and ran until I caught him.

"*Please* do not squash it" I implored him.

"Why shouldn't I?" he laughed.

"Oh, please don't! It's for my mother and she's ill. Do give it back."

He gave it back to me and I raced home with one hand on top of the peach, which by the time I got there was very soft indeed. I gave it to my mother, and great was my delight to see her enjoy such a luxury. I had never tasted a peach, but whenever I see one now that incident comes to my mind.

One year as Easter time came near, I decided to make some hot cross buns. I told my sister and we agreed to give our parents a surprise. So, early on Good Friday we got up very quietly. I was going to make the buns and Kathleen was to help. We had no recipe, but I thought I knew how to make them.

First we had to light the fire so that the oven got hot. This usually took a long time. Once the fire was lit I started on the buns. I emptied some flour into a bowl and put in a few currants, mixing them together with cold water until they made a stiff mixture. I dropped dollops of it on to a baking tin and put it in the oven. We stoked that fire, but the buns would not rise. They didn't even look like buns. By this time we knew that Mother and Father would soon be wanting their breakfast. This thought put me in a panic. I opened the oven door to look at the buns, took them out, burned my fingers in doing so and dropped the lot. My sister and I laughed until our tummies ached. My mother came and asked us what we thought we were doing. I told her of my efforts and asked her where I had gone wrong. Smiling, she reminded me that I had forgotten to put in the fat. This was my first and last attempt at making hot cross buns, but we did have some that day because Mother sent us to the baker to buy a few.

One day, because Mother was still unwell, I was kept home from school to help with the housework and dinner. My mother would give me instructions from her bed and I would clean and dust and make dinner for my father, my brothers and my sister. While I was cleaning I found some pictures, which to me looked very pretty. Now I must first tell you that owing to the vermin which infested the place Father would not allow anything at all to hang on the walls. I was unaware of this at the time, and so I decided to hang the pictures in my mother's bedroom. Its window faced a high warehouse, and as she lay in bed she could see nothing but brick walls. And all day long she heard little but the noise of carts rumbling by, cranes at work and men shouting. I cleaned and polished those pictures, found some nails and hung them up. It made a world of difference to that drab room.

Alas, neither my joy nor my mother's was to last long. On coming home to tea, my father went into my mother's bedroom. I stood waiting for his smile of pleasure. I quite thought he would like my efforts to cheer things up. But no! He immediately took a knife and cut the pictures down, telling me he would have *nothing* hanging on the walls. In vain we protested but, in quite a kindly manner, he pointed out that it was better so, as the pictures would soon be infected with vermin, which would make matters worse than they were already. I saw his point and agreed with him, but I was a very disappointed child that day.

CHAPTER FOURTEEN

My Brothers—Robert and William

AT THIS TIME the streets were very poorly lit at night. There were gas lamps that were lit each evening by the lamp-lighter. He carried a long pole which he used to pull a small chain which was attached to the lamp. Even when lit, these lamps gave a very poor light and we did not often go out after tea.

My eldest brother, Robert, was sometimes allowed to play outside in the evenings. It was a craze among the boys to make themselves carts, usually from a box and a pair of pram wheels. They added a couple of shafts and one boy would sit in the box while another pulled him along. One evening someone had the bright idea of putting lamps on the carts. Now a lamp cost twopence, plus a farthing for a candle. All the boys had one except Robert. On his return one evening, my father noticed that Robert's cart too had a lamp. He asked him how he had come by it.

Robert replied that one of his friends had given him the money with which to buy it. Father did not believe him. He put on his coat and took Robert to the boy's house, where he enquired if he had given my brother any money for the lamp. The boy said he had not. When they came home my father made Robert confess to having stolen the money with which he had bought both the lamp and the candle. In vain did he explain that all the other boys had lamps and that he was the only one without one. His words had no effect on Father, who determined that Robert must have a hiding. My mother pleaded with him not to do it, while we other children stood silent, afraid to speak. Finally Mother stood in front of Robert, trying to shield him from my father. This so angered him that he pushed my mother away and took Robert into the bedroom, locking the door after him. He made him strip and gave him a terrible beating with the belt he wore round his waist. I shall never forget Robert's cries or my mother's tears.

He was black and blue with bruises next morning and Mother did not speak to my father for many days after that. Such a hiding for such a small offence! I do not think Robert ever forgave my father. As he grew up there was always a coldness between them and many years afterwards, when Father was quite old, Robert did not even visit him.

So far I have not told you much about my brother William. Well, he was the middle of the three boys, quiet, thoughtful and very fond of horses. Every Saturday and most days during the holidays would find him in the yard of a cartage contractor, where the great carthorses pulled the carts away to their various destinations. The horses first had to be fed and watered, their harnesses made comfortable and their brasses cleaned, for the carmen were very proud of their animals' appearance. William would offer his help in return for a ride, but not many of the men would let him help. He did manage to make friends with one of them and was delighted when allowed to rub his horses down and clean the harnesses. The man repaid him by taking him on his cart. They passed through Poplar, where the carter lived. William was invited to lunch and proved himself to be such a help that each time he had a holiday this particular man would take him with him on his journeys. He would come home smelling of horses, which was most unpleasant, but, as my mother said, it was worth putting up with the smell to see him so happy.

As everyone knows, boys are always hungry—and William was no exception. We had tea at five o'clock and were allowed nothing more to eat until breakfast the next morning. We went to bed at seven o'clock and we never failed to ask for a slice of bread before we went. Mother would gladly have given it to us but Father would not allow it.

One evening after we had gone to bed, William came out of the bedroom into the kitchen where my father always sat during the evening. He said that he wanted to go to the toilet, which you will remember was just off the kitchen and enclosed in a small lobby where Mother kept the vegetables. William found a carrot, put it on his shoulder underneath his shirt and started to walk back to the bedroom. Of course, one shoulder looked higher than the other and my father noticed it at once. Tapping William's shoulder, he asked him what he was hiding. Out fell the carrot! My poor brother had a box round the ears and was sent back to bed in disgrace. In my mind's eye I can still see him, so upset that he cried himself to sleep.

I must tell you of the way we had to dispose of our rubbish. We did not have dustbins as you have today. As I mentioned, in each flat was a tiny lobby which housed the toilet, and in the wall of the lobby was a metal slide which opened wide enough for rubbish to be pushed through. This fell into a large container situated on the ground floor in the great yard below. If you lived on the ground floor, as we did, you sometimes had the most awful smells coming from the "shoot", as it was called. The container was emptied about once a fortnight and, as the dustmen pulled the rubbish out, great rats and mice would scamper out. Cats of every kind would have a feast on that day.

One day William had been out playing with his friends and I suspect they had raided a van, for he came home at tea-time with his jersey bulging with tomatoes. All his pockets were crammed with them too, in fact he was weighed down with tomatoes. He proudly emptied them on to the kitchen table, telling Mother that they were for her. I shall always remember her look when she turned to William and asked him where he had obtained them. He would not answer her and we all knew that he could not possibly have got such a quantity honestly. I remember that the whole family was in that afternoon except Father. Mother was a very honest woman and would go without rather than take what was not hers. Telling us to watch, she turned to William and asked him to open the slide which lead to the "shoot". She picked up the tomatoes one by one from the table and dropped them through the opening of the slide. Poor William! It was a hard lesson, but Mother explained that we must follow her example and never take that which did not belong to us. She promised not to tell Father and we children were too loyal to one another to tell him either.

CHAPTER FIFTEEN

How we Spent our Sundays

TRY, IF YOU WILL, to imagine what life was like all the week. Horses and carts rumbled all day long over the cobbled roads. The cranes on the warehouses squeaked and groaned as they loaded and unloaded the produce from the wharves. The smells of spices from the warehouses, men shouting, ships hooting: all was noise and hubbub. But on Sundays nobody worked. The ships were quiet, the warehouses shut, and the men home with their families.

As I have told you, there were no motor cars. On Sundays the streets were ours, and we could play safely on path or road. We would be dressed in our best clothes and sent to Sunday School both in the morning and the afternoon. In the evening we went to the lantern service. Kathleen and I each had one best dress, which was kept only for Sundays. We wore them to go to Sunday School in the morning, and on coming home it had to be taken off until it was time to set off for the afternoon session, when it would go on again. Returning home it would be taken off yet again until the evening lantern service. We had one pair of black stockings each, of a very poor quality. If they were washed too often they took on a greenish hue, so we had to take these off as well when we were not at church. We had to wear them for seven Sundays before Mother would wash them, in case they went a bad colour. We each had a straw hat in summer, which cost 1s. 11d. They were splendid hats, trimmed with wreaths of flowers. Our hair was plaited into two long pigtails all the week, but on Sundays we wore it hanging loose. We both had lovely hair, long and brown, and it looked very pretty on Sundays when we wore it tied with a ribbon. Even the ribbon was put away until the next week.

Our Sunday School was an old corrugated tin building known as the Tin Chapel. Nearly every child went, mainly to be out of their parents' way. I shall always remember trying to sit next to one girl from a rather

30

better-off family. She wore a muff. We did not even have the luxury of gloves, so you can imagine the envy I felt when I saw that muff.

"If only I could sit next to her and put my hands into that muff," I thought. I did manage to do it once and sat throughout one service with my hands warm inside, feeling like a queen. It is strange how such a small thing stays in the mind, yet things that happened just a few weeks ago are already forgotten.

In my young days, Sunday was observed as the Sabbath, at least by my mother. We went to Sunday School, but could not go out to play. We soon tired of this, so Kathleen and I would each conceal a ball in the leg of our knickers and go further away from home so that we could not be seen. We mostly walked to the Tower of London, bouncing our balls and having great fun as we went along. On reaching the entrance to the Tower, we would hide our balls and walk very sedately through the gate. You passed a "Beefeater" who let you through if you behaved. Once through the gates, you could see the cannons set at intervals pointing towards the river. These had been used in former days to defend the Tower. We passed Traitors' Gate where, in olden days, traitors were taken through on their way to execution. Then there were the sentries to watch as they marched up and down, smart in their scarlet jackets and dark trousers with a scarlet band down each side. Each wore a very large fur hat called a "bearskin". They really looked most impressive. Sometimes we could see the ravens which lived there. You could also see Tower Bridge spanning the river and on the Thames itself were ships, tugs and barges. Once, on a special day, we saw the Crown Jewels and visited the Armoury. Both were closely guarded. We looked as we walked by, but we were not allowed to stop. The Crown Jewels were most beautiful to see.

This then was our usual Sunday walk. We could not stay too long as we had to be home in time for afternoon Sunday School and we were never allowed to miss that. Sunday was for being good, at least that is what Mother told us.

I recall that we were taken one day for a tour of the Royal Mint, which stood almost opposite the Tower of London. It was a very large enclosed building with a small pond in front, which was full of goldfish. We had often watched the fish when on our walks, but didn't dream we would ever go inside the building where all the money was made. (By money I mean coins, for I do not think paper money was in circulation then.) Once inside we were amazed to see men stripped to the waist in front of large furnaces. We saw pennies and silver coins pouring into large containers. There was a barrier where we walked while watching this going on. How we longed to be given just one new penny and quite thought they couldn't possibly miss a few. But we were ushered out with nothing, much to our disappointment.

Some Sunday evenings in summer, Father and Mother would go to the Great Assembly Hall in the Mile End Road where services were held. The hall was an hour's walk from home and they went on foot both there and back to save the price of the tram fare. Long queues of down-and-outs gathered outside the hall before the service. They were dirty, homeless people who knew they would be given tea on condition that they stayed to attend the service. For them, starving and homeless, a free tea was indeed a great treat and often they would queue outside the hall all afternoon, waiting for the doors to open.

I sometimes went with my parents to these services, and I would sit and look at these wretched creatures, wondering how they came to be in such a condition. They had to sit up in the gallery, away from the rest of the congregation. Such itching and scratching you never saw. They must have been alive with vermin, so much did they scratch. It quite fascinated me to watch them. The preacher usually spoke of the Love of God and how he cared for all his children, and I often wondered what kind of God he could be that he was content to let these wretches remain as they were. I was only a child but already I was beginning to realise that people fell into different classes: the rich, the poor, and the un-washed. To me it simply didn't make sense. The people in the gallery were the unwashed. Some slept in lodging houses, some in doorways, wrapped in newspaper. Others huddled together for warmth under the railway arches. We would see them shuffling along with all their worldly possessions tied around their necks or fastened to their waists. They looked neither to right or left, for they had no interest in life, and no one cared whether they lived or died.

You may think this an exaggerated description of their condition, but I was there and I saw them. And although I now suspect that much of their plight was of their own making, I know that I was sorry for them at the time.

The singing during the services at the hall was very stirring. My father particularly enjoyed it and would return home cheerful and happy. He would sing around the house for the rest of the evening. Then back he went into his shell, and was tired and grumpy once again.

If he did not go to the hall then he used to lie down on the bed for a rest. I clearly remember coming home from Sunday School one afternoon and, forgetting that he was likely to be lying down, rushing into his bedroom for something, singing "The Cuckoo is a Pretty Bird" at the top of my voice. Before I could get further than the first line I was given a resounding smack on my face. I had woken Father up, and that was unforgivable. Since that incident, whenever I hear that particular song, the memory of that Sunday afternoon comes vividly to my mind.

✳ ✳ ✳ ✳ ✳

CHAPTER SIXTEEN

Sunday School Outing

THE SUNDAY SCHOOL OUTING was the one event of the year which we all looked forward to. You were only allowed to go if you had attended regularly, and as we had never missed a single week we always went. Sometimes we would go to Redhill or Epsom Downs, or even to Epping Forest. It didn't matter to us where we were taken, because it was a day in the country. We had to go to the Tin Chapel the evening before to receive our tickets, which we had to have sewn on to our clothes. It had our name and address on it and if it were not sewn on, we were not permitted to go.

We all gathered outside the Sunday School on the morning of the outing, each with his packet of sandwiches. Two big boys would carry between them a large banner bearing the words "Wesleyan East End Mission". Then came the band, made up of a dozen or so boys who belonged to the Boys' Brigade. After we had been arranged in pairs the band would start up and we marched through the streets to its music. Oh, it was wonderful! The day was ours, the sun shone and the band played. Every door was opened and every parent was there to wave us goodbye. You would have thought we were going for a year instead of one day. We sang all the way until we reached the train, and once aboard it we sang again. Nothing could dampen our spirits.

Dear reader, you cannot imagine what a day in the country meant. When we arrived we were let loose in a large field. We always made one wild rush to pick the buttercups and daisies which grew there in abundance. We would fill our hands with great bunches of them, but before very long we threw them away because we had so many other things to do and so many places to explore. There were trees to climb, frogs to catch and, best of all, tea at three o'clock. We all sat on the grass and we were each given a large paper bag containing jam sandwiches, a currant bun, a scone and a cake. Then we were given a large mug of tea. Great was the competition to see who could drink the most.

When it was time to go home, my sister and I would pick grasses until between us we had collected a large bunch. We took this home to our mother, who would welcome it as if it were some rare flower. The grasses would be put into a vase and, believe it or not, kept until the following year's outing, when they would be replaced by a fresh bunch.

✳ ✳ ✳ ✳ ✳

CHAPTER SEVENTEEN

Street Cries

ON SUNDAY AFTERNOONS we would hear the Muffin Man as he came down the street, ringing his bell and calling "Muffins and Crumpets". He wore a green baize apron and carried his wares on his head, in a tray covered with a white cloth. These were a great treat on winter evenings when we toasted them in front of the fire. Then came the shrimp and winkle man. Most people would buy something from him for their Sunday tea. Another man came selling celery, which he washed in a basin of water which he carried on his barrow. If it was not washed people would not buy it. Then there was watercress at one halfpenny a bunch and, during the season, mussels would be sold from a barrow at twopence a quart. These in particular were great delicacies.

We did not see these people on weekdays, but we had our daily callers as well. There was a man who came about four o'clock each day selling smoked haddock. We knew him as Swannee, from his cry of "Swannee Haddock". His fish was always good and cheap although sometimes it was broken. But then you could not expect whole fish to be as cheap as Swannee's were. Then there were the Italians who made their own ice cream and sold it from their brightly painted barrows, each of which

34

held two drum-shaped containers. Inside one was proper ice cream and in the other flavoured water-ice. Both these were served with a wooden scoop and put on to paper squares, which you held in your hand while licking the ice cream off with your tongue. For a halfpenny you could buy some of the water-ice, and with it went a little piece of lemon. We considered it a great treat even if it wasn't very hygienic. But then we did not think much about hygiene in those days.

Nearly everyone relied on these callers as there were so few shops, but the main reason for buying from them was because their goods were very cheap. I nearly forgot the paper-man: we were all very fond of him. He had a small barrow covered with a roof. It put you in mind of Noah's Ark. Into this barrow he put the Sunday papers. At about ten o'clock on Sunday mornings he would arrive outside the tenements and shout "Paper!" We children would go and get whatever paper our parents wanted. If somebody on the top floor wanted a paper, the man would send one of us with it and after we came down he would give us a comic which was a week or a fortnight old. We often did this for him because only in this way could we receive a coveted comic. Father would never allow one to be bought, saying it was a waste of money.

These are only little incidents but I hope they give you some idea of things which gave us pleasure. You might think it was not much fun to go up six flights of stone stairs with only an old comic for reward, but even that was enjoyed because we did not walk down six flights—we did better than that—we slid down on our bottoms, which was great fun!

Sunday was also the day when the beggars came. They were mostly men without homes, who slept in lodging houses in or around nearby Cable Street. We would hear the first one at about the same time as the paper-man arrived. He came walking in the middle of the road, singing hymns or playing a concertina. Father would never give him a penny, saying "Let him work. I do." We children would go and watch him and he would first do the High Street, then every little street and alley in turn so that he did not miss any. Next came a blind beggar with a placard around his neck, stating that he had a wife and four children. He had with him a small dog. This blind man would also sing. Father said he was a sham, only living off other people. Sometimes a woman came, wheeling a pram with two small children in it. How I wished I was rich, then I would have given them all something. Whether or not they were shams I shall never know. I only remember that at the time they had my sympathy.

CHAPTER EIGHTEEN

School Days

WHEN WE WERE CHILDREN there were no mixed schools in Wapping. My sister and I went to a board school, which was about a mile from home. To get there we had to pass many wharves and warehouses. On one side of the tenements stood a great tea warehouse. There was a coffee shop next to it with a large sign outside which read "A Good Pull Up For Car Men". The men who drive the carts which the horses pulled could get a good meal there. On the other side of the coffee shop was a cork warehouse and next to this was the boys' school. Walking past this one came to a spice warehouse, where all kinds of spices were blended. We always ran by this very quickly as the smells in the air made us sneeze. On the far side was one of the dock bridges. At high tide it was opened to let the ships in and out of the docks.

On either side of the bridge facing the river were large important-looking houses, where the Dockmaster and the other high officials lived. Then came the Rectory and the church with its clock and adjoining charity school, where children were given clothing if they attended church on Sundays and school all week. My mother was too proud to send us to a charity school so we went to the board school. Past the church there were two wharves: one for storing great crates of bananas, and another for sugar. Right next to the sugar wharf was a soap factory. This sent out some very unpleasant odours when the soap was actually being made but most of the time the smells were varied and delightful.

Then at last came the school. It was an old two-storied building with a mean little playground and surrounded by tenement buildings. I remember hating school in winter because I was always cold. True, there was always a nice fire in each classroom, but I never felt its warmth because I had to sit at the back of the class. How I envied the girls who sat in front! But only the naughty ones sat there so that the teacher could keep her eye on them.

We had a dear Headmistress, whom we called "Governess". I loved her very much for she had been my mother's Governess in her school days. She seemed quite old to me. She was always kind and understanding. After I left school I often went to visit her and she never failed to welcome me.

I recall a most unhappy time when my father came to the conclusion that I needed a lesson. Now you may understand, as I do now, how hard it must have been to keep a family of five children neat and tidy. We all wore boots, shoes being only for the well-to-do. It happened that I wore mine out much too quickly for my father's liking. True, I would slide behind the carts as they went along, and kick and dance as any child would, but the fact was I wore my boots out more quickly than did my sister and brothers. One Saturday Father took me to get a new pair. How pleased I was to be getting a new pair before the others! We entered the shop and my father asked for a pair of *boy's* boots to fit me. In vain I cried, telling him I would be more careful if only I could have girl's boots, but my tears had no effect on him and boy's boots I had, fitted with tips and blakeys. As soon as we got home he put studs in the soles. Oh! the noise they made. I felt terrible. The other children laughed, and I cried myself to sleep for many nights. Those boots would *not* wear out. I kicked with them and I slid with them. In fact I did my utmost to make them wear out, but they would not. At last I grew out of them and they were handed down to one of my brothers. I need not tell you that this lesson taught me to be more careful with my next pair of girl's boots!

CHAPTER NINETEEN

A New School

I MUST HAVE BEEN about eleven years old when my mother received a note from my school Governess saying I had been selected to go to a higher grade school as I was considered to be "bright". Mother was very pleased for me and set about getting the school uniform of navy gym slip, white blouse and large straw hat, with the school badge on it. The gym slip was meant to reach to the knees but my father insisted on it being longer and larger, so that I could grow into it. When I put it on it nearly reached my ankles, but I had to wear it and I felt awful.

On arrival at the school, the new pupils were sent together to see the Headmaster. He asked me to stay behind. When the others had left he told me my slip was much too long and I would have to have it shortened.

I explained that my father had said I must wear it this length and that he would not have it shortened. I remember the Headmaster saying "Poor child" as he sent me to my classroom. I was laughed at by the other children, who were mostly Jewish and came from better-off homes than I did. I was named "Polly Long Frock". I found it difficult to concentrate and failed my exams.

At this time Father was out of work and free dinner tickets were given to the children of poor families. One day at Assembly, the Headmaster asked who needed a dinner ticket. Imagine my dismay when I saw I was the only person to put up a hand. I had to walk to the front of the whole school to receive this ticket, which enabled me to have dinner at a centre for poor children, near to the school. I felt too ashamed to go and so during the dinner break I would walk the surrounding streets. I did not tell my mother this but she found out because one day I met a man who knew my father. He asked me what I was doing walking about when I should have been having my dinner. Tearfully I poured it all out to him. He felt very strongly about what I told him, for he was very fond of me. He took me to a nearby coffee-shop where we both had a hearty meal. Later he came to see my parents and told them all about it before going to see the Headmaster to ask that dinner tickets be given in private to children who needed them. This change was eventually made, but I still continued to be a most unhappy child while at this school.

One day, during a lesson on the meaning of words, the teacher—a man—asked me the meaning of a word and I gave the wrong answer. He shouted "Sit down, you big-eyed goon!" The other children thought it funny, but I felt stupid and unhappy. When I went home that evening I pleaded with my mother and father to allow me to go back to my old school again. Mother went to see my former Governess, who said she would have me back. How happy I was, back among my own kind. I worked much better there, and got very good marks.

Such were the joys and sorrows of my childhood.

B.H.W. D

CHAPTER TWENTY

The Games we Played

As I HAVE TOLD YOU, we had no garden to play in, so we spent most of the time in the streets. As the seasons changed so did the games. In winter Kathleen and I would each have a skipping rope; this was a piece of ship's rope, there being no other kind. How we skipped and jumped through that rope! We took it everywhere with us and had great fun inventing different skipping games. We held hands crossed behind our backs and galloped along pretending to be bus-horses. But when the better weather came we played hopscotch, marbles and gobs and bonsters. We all had tops. The boys would have peg tops which they could spin with the aid of a piece of string. The girls had whip tops which were whipped every few minutes to keep them going. We made the whips from lengths of string attached to pieces of cane or wood.

Then there was diabolo, in which the game was to send a wooden top spinning through the air from a string attached to two sticks. As it came down you sent it spinning up again. This required great skill and I was never able to do it. The best game of all was "Knocking Down Ginger". About a dozen of us would get into a line and run quickly along a street knocking at each door as we raced along. We must have been a great annoyance to the people who lived inside the houses but this was our favourite game and never once did we get caught.

In summer when it was hot, the boys would go down the shoreways and strip off all their clothing and bathe in the muddy water of the Thames. How we girls wished we too could go, but the boys would post one of their number on guard at the entrance to keep the girls away. This was strictly for boys only. They had no towels with which to dry themselves, but cheerfully dried off with their shirts. How we envied them but, being girls, how could we too enjoy this game? There was no answer to this, and the boys laughed to think they had scored over the girls.

CHAPTER TWENTY-ONE

The Cats and the "Cats-meat" Woman

I SUPPOSE I must have been born with more than my share of sympathy and pity for all living things, and have sometimes let my heart rule my head. But I am as I am and I don't suppose I shall change now. As I have told you, the tenements were infested with mice and rats and everybody kept a cat to help keep these pests at bay. When the cats got too old or they had too many kittens people would turn them out to fend for themselves. Most of them found their way into the great yard which lay behind the tenements, where they lived on anything they could find. People would throw out all unwanted scraps, including fish-heads and the like. The cats were truly starving. Many had mange and sores, and there were always dozens of kittens! I used to look at these poor creatures and think "How can people be so cruel?" My friend Winifred and I would often talk about these cats and we both decided that when we grew up we would open a Cats' Home. It would be called "The Winifred Home". One day I saw a cat with a salmon tin over its head. Someone had thrown it out and the poor creature, smelling fish, had put its head into the tin, and could not get it out again. The poor thing was going quite mad in its efforts to free itself. It never did, because next day I saw it lying in the yard quite dead.

Now I had heard of a place at Shadwell, about one-and-a-half hours walk from home, where unwanted cats could be taken, so each time I could entice a cat into our house I would put it into a large bag and carry it until I reached this place. I would then hand it in saying it was a stray. In this way I took many cats to this place. The neighbours found out and called me "Queen of the Cats". Word got around to the effect that if you wanted to get rid of a cat, Gracie would take it for you as a shilling was paid for each cat taken to Shadwell. That was a piece of pure invention on someone's part, and I only took them because I felt sorry for them!

There was no time during my childhood when we did not keep a cat. My mother would regularly put all the boots she could find on a chair beside her bed each night. As soon as it got quiet, out would come the mice; they would scamper about the room in a most alarming manner.

43

Every now and then we would hear a bang and we knew it was Mother throwing a boot at the place where the offending noise came from. This would scare the mice for a few minutes then they would come out again; she would throw all the boots until none were left. Then the nuisance would continue as before. Mother always kept a female cat as these were considered to be better "mousers". How we loved our cat. It was always having kittens. After a day or two they were taken away and drowned. This always upset my sister and I. On winter evenings when it was bedtime, I would quietly call the cat into the bedroom. We went to bed together, she purring happily and I stroking and loving her until we both fell asleep.

On looking out of the kitchen window one day I saw a sick cat lying in the great yard. I watched for a long time then I went out with a little milk and tried to feed it, but it would not take any. It lay there, not moving. I felt very concerned about it and wondered how I could make it better. I must have been very young and stupid, but I decided I must help this cat. I would take it to the Children's Hospital at Shadwell. I carefully put the cat in a box, covered it with my doll's blanket and made my way to Shadwell on foot. As you know, we had no transport of any kind. It was such a long journey, but I kept whispering to the cat that soon it would be much better. The box got heavier and heavier, but still I went on until I reached the hospital. I went to the Out-Patients Department and was asked who the patient was. I explained it was the cat and asked "Could you not make it better?" I think they thought I was quite mad, for they told me they had enough sick children without seeing after cats and if it was sick to take it to a cats' home. So I carried it home again and my mother let me nurse it all evening, but on waking in the morning I found the cat dead. My mother suspected it had been poisoned, but of course we never found out.

About twice a week we would see the "cats-meat" woman on her rounds. Most people who kept a cat would have a regular order with her for a halfpenny-worth of cats' meat. The woman was dressed in a long full skirt, a black straw hat, and black boots. Around her shoulders she wore a coloured woollen shawl and on her arm she bore a large basket in which she carried the meat, cut into small pieces and fixed on to wooden skewers. She charged one halfpenny per skewer. She came along calling out "Cats' meat!" Many cats, either smelling the meat or knowing the call, followed her as she went along. As she came to each house where she delivered, she got her meat out and fastened it under the door-knocker. I often saw cats jumping up the doors in an effort to reach the meat. People did not bother to take the meat from off the skewer. They gave it to the cats as it was as it took them longer to eat it this way.

CHAPTER TWENTY-TWO

The Church and our Clergyman's Wife

IF YOU WALKED down the High Street until you came to the Dock Bridge you only had to walk a little further and you came to Church Street. On one side was the churchyard and on the other the church, called St. John of Wapping, with its adjoining school. The church and the school were maintained with money left years before. Standing in an alcove were stone figures of a boy and girl dressed in the fashion of bygone days. The church was old, but quite lovely to my eyes; you walked up about a dozen steps to reach the entrance. On our way to school we could see the time by looking down Church Street. If the clock said twenty-to-nine, we knew we must hurry as we still had quite a way to go.

I had only been into the church once and knew nothing of how a church service was conducted. One of my friends went each Sunday evening and she asked me to go with her instead of going to our usual Sunday lantern service. I went with her. (Here I must tell you I was always a giggler. I would giggle at the most serious things. I don't know why I did it, but once I started I could not stop.) The service started with the choir boys walking down the centre of the church. They were wearing white robes with a pleated ruff round the neck. I thought they looked very funny and could not imagine why they were dressed in this fashion. Then the priest came into the pulpit. He too had on what seemed to be a large white nightgown. He was a fat man with a bald head and I wanted to laugh, but at that point the singing started and then everyone sat down while the priest prayed. I was most startled to hear the congregation chanting after he had stopped. Then he went on again. This went on and I couldn't understand what they were doing or why, and I started to giggle. I tried to stop, but each time the chanting came I giggled more. While the chanting was going on I could not be heard, but when it stopped and all else was quiet, I still continued to giggle. Everyone was shocked at such behaviour and the priest's wife, a lady called Mrs. Saint, got up and came to me. She took hold of my hand and escorted me to the door, telling me she would come and tell my mother about my shocking behaviour. This she did. My mother apologised for me, saying that it would not happen again and I was not allowed to go to church any more.

I really must say a good word for Mrs. Saint. Before coming to work in the church she had been a qualified doctor. As you know, many people could not afford a doctor and you would not call one in or go to one unless absolutely necessary. Mr. and Mrs. Saint lived at the Rectory which adjoined the churchyard. They employed a maid for the sole purpose of opening the door to the many callers. If anyone in our community had a sick or ailing child who did not respond to treatment at home, Mrs. Saint was the one to go to. We all knew she would advise or help in any way she could. She kept a special room as a consulting room and the hall was used as a waiting-room. It did not matter who you were, or whether you belonged to the church or not; it didn't make any difference, she would attend to anyone who cared to go and she made no charge for her advice (which in most cases was necessary). My mother took my youngest brother to her one day as she could not stop him screaming and, upon examining him, Mrs. Saint told her that he must go to hospital at once, as he had a rupture. My husband when a little boy, was very ill at home, so ill that his mother had to put him in a push cart to take him to see Mrs. Saint. This was on a Sunday morning when she should have been attending church, but she stopped to examine him and said he had pleurisy and must go to hospital. On arrival he was admitted and was ill for many days. I think Mrs. Saint must have been the means of saving many children's lives and I am sure you will think, as I do, that her name was most apt.

CHAPTER TWENTY-THREE

Beanos

EACH YEAR IN SUMMER every public house in our community would have its annual outing, known as a "Beano". All the year the men would pay into the Beano Club. Then, when the day came, there would be enough money for the treat. This was for men only and it was always held on a Sunday.

At about nine in the morning the brake would arrive. A brake was a vehicle with open sides and a canvas roof which could be rolled back in fine weather. Down each side were forms for sitting on. A pair of wooden steps would be placed at the back of the brake to allow the passengers to climb in. There were four large wooden wheels with iron rims on them. In front was the driver's seat. This was called the "dickey". It stretched the width of the brake. Sometimes the brake was drawn by two horses who were harnessed side by side with a wooden shaft in between to separate them. If the brake was large, four horses would be used, two more being placed in front of the first two already there. It required great skill to drive a brake with four horses, for they were controlled only by the pull of the reins held by the driver.

At about eight o'clock we would all gather to watch for the brake. All the men came dressed in their best clothes. Each would have his packet of sandwiches tied with a bright red or green handkerchief. Crates of beer would be loaded into the brake as soon as it arrived, and the men would climb in. The driver would get into his dickey seat and with him came the man who sat next to the driver and who always carried a cornet. When all was ready he would sound a loud fanfare.

This was the moment we had all been waiting for. With a great shout we would all call "Throw out your mouldies!" The men would have their pockets and hands full of coppers and as the brake started on its journey they would fling them into the roadway. You never saw such a scrambling and pushing in all your life. The children would fight and push, hoping to find a stray copper. My sister and I were always there to watch but I do not think we ever found a copper. We were much too afraid of the big boys. But it was fun to watch from a safe distance. I think this one day was the only outing most of these men had during the year. About eleven at night we would hear the sound of the cornet player as the men returned. Most of them were drunk but they sang and laughed as they set off coloured lights. All declared next day that they had had a wonderful time.

✳ ✳ ✳ ✳ ✳

CHAPTER TWENTY-FOUR

Hop-Picking

EVERY YEAR in the second week of September many people went hop-picking. Mostly they were women and children; men only went if they happened to be out of work at the time. Nearly all of them went to the Kent hopfields. It was a working holiday but it meant a change of surroundings, fresh air and freedom to enjoy the evenings when the day's work was finished. On the day they set off, the pickers would start out from Wapping about seven in the evening, walking to London Bridge Station, which was about two miles away. They were allocated a special train which left at midnight and there was usually a wait of a few hours on the station.

We would watch them as they went by. The things they took with them would have astounded you. They took pots and pans, bedding, toys, carts, prams and pushchairs loaded with every possible thing which they might need, for they stayed for six weeks. Nothing was provided for them except a truss of straw to lie on.

They slept in barns, outhouses or huts and all day they would pick hops. When meal-times came there was usually a Granny who could not pick but who could do the cooking. A fire would have to be made in the open and the meal cooked on this. Sticks and twigs would be gathered for the fire, and water carried from a well. There were no sanitary arrangements, except a bucket in a hut. It was a very rough life, but these people were tough and knew how to rough it and enjoy it as well. All would be expected to pick, but many children played truant, preferring to go scrumping in the farmers' orchards. And who could blame them, for here were things they never saw in Wapping.

All of them would come home laden with hopping apples, and a little extra money. We never went hopping but I always envied those among my friends who did. What I would have liked but never had was one of those lovely large juicy hopping apples!

CHAPTER TWENTY-FIVE

My Father Loses his Job and gets Another

I BELIEVE it was in 1912 that Father lost his job. The men working in the docks worked long hours and received very little pay. Much of the work was for casual labour. We would see groups of men outside a warehouse where a ship had berthed during the night. Here was work for the lucky. Some men were regular, but most of them relied for their work on the different ships coming in to the various docks and wharves and they were paid by the hour. The foreman would come out and beckon to as many men as he needed for the job. The men who were left standing would make a mad rush to the next warehouse in the hope of a day's work. I have seen men who were good friends fight each other for the privilege of getting the job.

Times were hard. The men were dissatisfied. Meetings were held and the men decided, aided by their Union, to strike for better conditions. This strike lasted for many weeks. The Union ran short of funds, but still neither side would give way. We had no money, no food and no hope. The men were desperate and the Army was called in to keep order. Soup kitchens were opened so that at least the children had one good meal a day. But not so the parents. They managed as best they could.

When winter came some kind friends belonging to the East End Mission gave breakfast to any child who cared to partake of it. Needless to say, every child went who could. The breakfast consisted of a mug of cocoa and two thick slices of bread and jam. We walked for half-an-hour to get it and half-an-hour back, then on to school where we each received our dinner ticket entitling us to our dinner at a soup kitchen. Father was a staunch Unionist and I believe encouraged the men where he worked to stick it out. When the strike was finally settled my father was called to the Manager's office and told he was no longer required as he was considered to be an agitator. This was indeed a blow as he had been there for twenty years. He was blacklisted wherever he went. No-one wanted an agitator. His work-mates avoided him in case they also got involved. Each man was too afraid of his own job to be his friend again. Father was indeed a marked man.

I so wanted to help him and then I had an idea. I would write to the

Manager and tell him how sorry my father was. This I did, quite thinking all would be forgiven, but I received no answer to my childish letter. Although I hoped and hoped for a reply none came, but eventually Father did get a job.

As I have already told you, there were many public houses in Wapping. In fact I do not think you could walk down any one of those narrow little streets without seeing one. They always seemed to be full of men and women. Children were not allowed in so they were left outside while their parents drank inside. Neither my father nor my mother drank, so this did not worry us children, except on Saturday nights, when there was more drinking than usual. There were no official closing times, so each Saturday night at about twelve o'clock we would be woken up by the noise of drunken men and women coming home from the pubs. There would be singing, dancing, swearing, fighting and drunken laughter. I believe this is why some well-meaning people got together and formed a Temperance Society for the parents and a Band of Hope for the children. Songs were written about the evils of strong drink, and each of the women who joined the Society was given a brooch made into the shape of a white bow, which she wore to indicate that she was teetotal.

We went to the Band of Hope for one evening each week, but we did not need to be told of the misery which strong drink could cause. It was all around us. Children went barefoot and ragged because of it. The few possessions these people had went each Monday morning to the pawnbroker to pay the rent. Even Sunday suits and boots were pawned for a shilling or two. This meant that people had nothing to wear but their working clothes, except on Sundays. You see, the clothes went in on Monday and were redeemed on Saturday, so all week long they had to wear the same clothes. Although my mother did not drink she joined the White Ribbon Brigade, as it was then called, just to encourage others to give up this destructive habit.

It was at about this time that Father lost his job. One of the well-to-do ladies who lived on the Pier Head heard about my father and the plight that we were in. Father was offered a job as a labourer with the Port of London Authority. The wages were small but it was work and we were happy once again. As Mother remarked to my father when he told her how little he would be earning, "Half a loaf is better than none".

But alas, the job did not last long. Father worked under the other men and one day when they wanted to brew some tea he was sent by them to find some. If you are not familiar with dock life you will not know the temptations which surrounded men on every side. At home you had to pay twopence for a packet of tea, while at work there were cases of it by the hundred. So do not blame those men if they pilfered a bit here and there. Well, on this occasion Father went and pilfered enough tea to brew a pot, and on the way back he was stopped by a dock policeman. Father was sacked on the spot for stealing. In a community such as ours this was indeed a disgrace and it was many days before my mother could bring herself to go out. I think she felt worse than anyone about it. But (as is the way with children) we were soon out and about again, with not a care in the world.

This was what we were born into, and we knew no world outside it. We made our own childish pleasures and were happy.

✳ ✳ ✳ ✳

CHAPTER TWENTY-SIX

Local Characters

As CHILDREN WE KNEW everyone around the area where we lived, but I suppose it is natural for some of them to stand out in my mind more than others. I recall that we had one policeman, who kept order. He was a very large man with big feet and a big nose. I don't remember his proper name, but we could always give a name to anybody and we called him Bootnose. If we were doing anything we shouldn't and one of us saw him approaching, we would shout "Bootnose!" This one word would send us all rushing through the first street or alley we came to.

Then I remember a short, fat man who earned his living by rowing men from the shoreways to their ship, lying mid-river. He owned a small wooden rowing-boat in which he spent most of the day. His nose was very red, with a large growth on either side giving the impression that he really had three noses stuck together. With the cold logic of children, we named him Old Three Noses.

Children can be very cruel when they are small. There was one poor woman who was a widow. She was quite an inoffensive creature, but was nearly always partly intoxicated. She would walk unsteadily, reeling this way and that. She interfered with no-one, but each time we children saw her we would shout out at her; we called her Old Mother Born-Drunk. How we tormented her, not realising how cruel we were being!

We had another character who kept a small sweet shop, a surly, grumpy man. He was a cripple and walked with a limp. I expect he must have suffered quite a bit from the remarks of us children. We knew he could not run so we stood at a safe distance and shouted "Grumpy Lloyd" and by this name he became known. (I hope I do not bore you, but I'd like you to know that I was as naughty as the rest and really enjoyed these childish games.)

I nearly forgot one character that I feel you would like to know about; this was the local chimney sweep. His name was Mr. Kelly. He was a tall, thin man who was a widower and when he was not sweeping chimneys he spent his time in the pub. You may think "What a lot of time people spent in pubs in those days", but there was no other place for a man to go. The chimneys of the tenements had to be swept every six weeks in winter. So badly built were they that you could not have a fire if you did not have it swept that frequently. The smoke would pour into the room and you were almost choked by it. Mr. Kelly had a standing order to come every six weeks to sweep ours. He would always promise to come early but he very seldom arrived until late afternoon, after the pubs had closed. He would put the rods up the chimney until he reached halfway, at which point the chimney must have curved or sloped for he always had a terrific job to get them to go up higher. Then he would curse and swear and say all manner of things about that chimney. When he thought he had managed to get it through to the pot at the top of the building, he would make us go and see if the brush really was out. His charge for this dirty and tiring job was ninepence.

One day, on hearing him swear so much, I asked him if it made the rods go up more easily if he swore at them. He stood for a while looking at me, then asked me why I wanted to know. I told him that it was wicked to swear; my mother would not allow us to, so why did he?

"I'll tell you what" he said. "When I come next time you remind me not to swear, than I shan't forget." He came many more times and he would always greet me with "I'm not swearing, at least not in *your* home!"

Most days in summer and winter we would see the man who played the barrel-organ. This was a musical instrument with two wheels and two handles. The man would push it whenever he wanted to play. When he turned the handles it played the popular songs of the day. On weekdays the songs were gay and cheerful and we would follow him around singing and dancing to the music. But on Sundays he would play hymns and sacred music. He mostly played outside the public houses for here he would collect more money—and that of course was why he played it. I often pitied this man. He was quite old, and very tall and thin. I often wondered where he lived. One day quite by chance I found out.

In those days the Salvation Army women had just started to visit people to sell "The Young Soldier", their weekly paper. One of these Salvationists called at our house trying to sell us her little paper. I think it cost one penny. This led to her visiting us each week. She would tell us of the social side of the work, which interested me very much. Seeing my interest she invited me to go with her one day to visit an old man and woman who were so poor that she went as often as she could to take them soup, which was made by the Salvationists. I went with her and to my surprise found that the old man was the barrel-organist. He lived in one room above a shop, with his wife, a tiny little old woman, nearly bent in half with age. The room was bare except for an old table, two chairs and an old bed. There were no blankets for the bed. Overcoats were used to cover them in winter. I was very shocked on seeing this and when I told my mother she said "One half of the world has no idea of how the other half lives." Whenever I had a chance I would visit this old couple and chat with them. I learned that the man had been a school-teacher in his younger days but ill-health had forced him to give it up. They existed in this one room and he would go out in all weathers to earn a little by playing his barrel-organ. We who are growing old have much to be thankful for, for people care about us, but this couple were only one example of how the old were neglected when I was young.

Jenny had come from Scotland to live among us with her mother, a widow who earned her living by cleaning city offices. Jenny was a lovely girl with red hair and a soft lilting voice. She came to school with us and we loved to hear her speak in her Scottish accent. As she grew older she met, and later married, Tony. Tony opened a fish-and-chip shop just around the corner from the tenements. It was a great success. We had had no fish-and-chip shop before this one and each evening you would see crowds of children waiting for Tony to open. Then they would all crowd in shouting "a halfpenny piece and a halfpennyworth of chips". You got a nice sized piece of fish and a paper full of chips for one penny. If you only had one halfpenny you could get a halfpennyworth of "crackling", the small pieces of batter which fell off the fish as it was cooking. Jenny would serve you with a large newspaperful. Jenny had lots of babies and they would be in the shop with her as she served. If one of her children needed something while she was serving she would keep everybody waiting while she attended to him. But nobody minded waiting, for we would watch Tony cutting the fish and dipping it into the batter. Besides, it was warm in the shop and we had fun with each other while we waited. Mind you, if we became too noisy Jenny would turn us out, so we all knew just how far we could go. Tony was quiet and never spoke to us. I don't think he could speak much English, and that was the reason for his quietness. Jenny's mother would sometimes help with the babies, for she lived there with them. Poor Jenny, I don't think she ever had any time off from serving. Tony did not employ anyone else. She seemed suddenly to become old, then she became ill and died. Tony closed down the fish shop and went away. We were all sorry to see the shop close. Some other people opened it up afterwards, but it was never the same after Jenny had gone.

Charlie was a bachelor about fifty years old, who kept the sweet shop next to Tony. He was rather grubby and untidy and lived with two cats which he allowed to sit on the counter among the toffees. They were female cats and were always having kittens. We liked to go to Charlie's. He would give you good weight for your farthing. He sold egg-and-milk toffee, tiger nuts, Polish nuts, tamerans and such sweets as we do not see today. He also sold hot drinks. He put a small drop of fruit essence into a glass and then filled it up with hot water from a kettle. This was nice, especially in the winter when he would let you stay in the shop with your drink, which only cost you a halfpenny. I think he was glad of anyone's company, for he lived alone in one room at the top of the house. We did not have many shops, but I think Charlie's was the favourite.

We had one baker's shop in our community, owned and run by a German and his wife. They had a family of four children. They baked their bread on the premises and sold it by weight. Each loaf was two pounds. It was weighed when purchased and if the scales showed it to be a little underweight, a nice piece of bread pudding would be added to make the weight up. This we called "make-weight"; and we were allowed to eat it on the way home. The bread was good and crusty and everybody dealt there. The baker and his family were kindly, homely folk and we all liked them.

B.H.W. I

One day, after the shop was closed they went for a walk, then for a tram ride to Whitechapel Road to look at the shops. They were making their way back to the tram when they saw a parcel in a doorway. On picking it up they discovered it was a tiny baby girl. They took her home, bathed and fed her and kept her for their own. We were all very thrilled when we saw the baby and ever after she was known as " Lambie " and lived as one of their family. Yet these were the people who were stoned when war came; these were our neighbours, yet they were cast out because of their nationality.

Life was never dull when I was young. There was always something interesting to see or do. One of my greatest pleasures was to watch the farrier at work. There were many carthorses in Wapping and only one farrier. So every man took his horse there to be shod. The farrier worked in a great open shed. Here he had a large fire, over which he heated the iron until it was red hot. Then he took a large hammer and holding the iron with a large pair of pincers he would hammer it, bending and shaping it until he had made a horse-shoe. Then he fitted it on to the hoof of the horse, who stood by while all the preparations were going on. If the shoe did not fit he heated it again and hammered it into exactly the right shape. Then with another tool he made the holes into which the nails went. When all was ready, he took a hot iron and, lifting up the horse's leg, he would burn the hoof a little to make it smooth so that the shoe fitted perfectly. I used to watch and wonder, thinking that this must be painful to the horse, but I was assured that this did not hurt because the hoof was hard and horny and had no feeling in it of any kind. When shod like this the horse made quite a noise when he walked. As there were a great many horses there was also a great deal of noise! Alas, these are no more. All we hear nowadays is the noise of cars and lorries. The horses were quiet by comparison.

CHAPTER TWENTY-SEVEN

Christmas and After

IN THE VERY EARLIEST DAYS of my childhood, Christmas was the happiest time of the whole year. Father was in regular employment at that time of my life and always saved for Christmas. On Christmas Eve we would have an early tea before Father took Robert and me with him to Smithfield Market, which was about an hour's walk from home. There we would see turkeys, geese, ducks and chickens being auctioned by stall-holders. There were a great many fruit stalls as well and Father would go to each one in turn to see who was selling the cheapest. He usually bought a large turkey which cost about twenty-five shillings. Having got this he would then buy twenty-five oranges for a shilling. Then came the nuts. I do not remember the cost of these but he bought 1 lb. of each. On we went to the sweet stall. There were so many kinds of boiled sweets, all priced at 4 ozs for one penny. He would buy 1 lb. of mixed ones and a box of Turkish Delight. We would wander from stall to stall, sometimes feeling so cold that Robert and I secretly wished we hadn't come, but Father wanted us with him to help carry back the heavy load. We carried a bag each and cheered ourselves up by talking about the next day, which would be Christmas Day.

When we arrived home Mother would be waiting, happy and smiling and with supper ready—a great treat, for it was the one night of the year when we were allowed to have it. Of course we hung our stockings up. Just a stocking, but it held all we would receive. Needless to say we woke early on Christmas morning to look into our stockings. For Kathleen and me there was usually a doll each. Hers had dark hair and mine fair. My father had bought these dolls at the street market which was held each Sunday morning in Petticoat Lane and they cost 1s. 11d. each. They were lovely dolls, "double-jointed", which meant that they could move all their joints, including wrists and ankles. They also opened and shut their eyes. But, best of all, they were dressed—even to a hat. The doll was the only toy in our stocking. We expected no more. The rest of the stocking contained a few nuts, some sweets, a bag of chocolate money, a sugar mouse, and at the bottom was a bright new penny.

Breakfast was special on Christmas Day. It would be sausages and tomatoes which had been purchased while at the market. Dinner was wonderful, the turkey with sage-and-onion stuffing, baked potatoes and cabbage. And then came the Christmas pudding which we had all helped to make weeks before. No puddings ever tasted as good as these.

After dinner we played with our new toy while Father and Mother cleared away. For tea we had celery or whatever had been cheapest to buy at the time, but there was never a Christmas cake. We had never had one and didn't expect it. No Christmas tree either. They were for the wealthy. But we were content with what we had.

In the evening we would gather round the fire while my father roasted chestnuts, which was another great treat. We ate a whole orange each, had one or two sweets and played Happy Families together. You must remember we had to make our own pleasures, for there was no wireless, television, tape-recorder or the like. Our pastimes were simple and mostly make-believe. These indeed were happy days, and I shall always treasure them.

After Christmas, if we had been extra good and helpful and there was enough money left over, Father would take Robert and me, the eldest children, to see a Pantomime. The Panto was held in a Music Hall in Shoreditch. It was called the "Shoreditch Olympia". I believe it cost fourpence to go into the Gallery, which was at the top of the Hall and consisted of wooden planks with no backs to them. We climbed many stairs to reach it. It was hard and uncomfortable but we could see everything that went on. There were no loudspeakers or microphones in those days but we generally managed to hear what was being sung or spoken. We saw "Babes in the Wood", "Aladdin", "Robinson Crusoe" and many others. Once we saw "Alibaba and the Forty Thieves" but I didn't enjoy that. At one part in the performance the stage was covered with barrels and as the play went on, suddenly the supposed thieves, who had been concealed in the barrels, sprang out. This frightened me very much, but my brother was most amused. We loved the Pantomime, the bright lights, the colours and the singing but I never could understand why the men actors dressed as ladies and the ladies as men!

From Shoreditch to Wapping was a very long way. We could have a halfpenny tram ride when we were about halfway home but we always walked all the way there and back, because about halfway home there would be a Hot Potato Man. He had a small barrow with a coke fire, on which he baked potatoes in their jackets. You could get a large one sprinkled with salt, piping hot for a halfpenny. If we had the tram ride we couldn't have the potato. Father would let us choose which we should have. We always chose the potato and ate it going home. No potatoes ever tasted so good or were enjoyed so much. It meant an hour's walk to have it, but we considered it to be the better buy.

✻ ✻ ✻ ✻ ✻

CHAPTER TWENTY-EIGHT

A Country Holiday

I DO NOT KNOW how it came about, but at school one day we were asked if any of us would like to go to the country for a fortnight. The cost would be 2s. 1d. each. If we wanted to go we could pay into the penny bank which was held at school. You could pay a penny or more, as you could afford it. My parents consented to my sister and I going and each week on Monday morning in went our precious pennies, until we had enough to pay for both of us to go. My mother patched and altered and sewed until she was satisfied we had enough clothes to last us the fortnight. I think about twelve children went in all. We travelled by train to a place called Childrey. I do not remember what county it was in, but I recall it as a small village consisting of only a few cottages. On arrival at the small country station we were met by a group of country women, who looked us over and then chose which child she would take. I refused to go with any of them unless Kathleen came too. I had been told to look after her as she was younger than I. Now each woman had expected to take only one child and had room for no more. There we stood, refusing to be separated, until a kindly woman came and said she would have us if we did not mind being crowded a bit.

Great was our relief to know that somebody wanted us. She took us home to her small cottage. There was the kitchen in which we all lived, and two bedrooms upstairs, one for her and her husband and one for the children. She had three girls of about our age with whom we shared a large double bed. This was contrived by putting the two of us at the wrong end of the bed. We had great fun sleeping five in one bed.

On the first night we were greatly surprised to see them undress and get into bed with no nightdresses. They in turn were most amused to see us put ours on. They asked us what they were, for they had never worn

such things and always stripped all their clothes off before tumbling into bed. Nightdresses were unheard of in that family.

I must not forget to tell you that there was another member of the household: a small lively little dog called Poppy, with whom we had great fun. At our first breakfast there I could not believe it, for there on the table on each plate was a large brown egg. This may be surprising to you, but we had never eaten a whole egg before. Only my mother had an egg in our house and the lucky one among us children had the top of the egg before she dipped into the yolk. So you can imagine how much we enjoyed an egg to ourselves.

The cottage stood in a very big piece of ground, which seemed to us children to begin and end nowhere. There were fruit trees, fruit bushes and so many flowers, which nobody ever tended but which were all beautiful. There were chickens, and a goat of which we were very frightened. We were allowed anywhere in the garden and I well remember finding a large gooseberry bush which was covered with delicious fruit. I sat down and I ate my fill. I think I almost stripped that bush, for here was the first fruit I had ever seen growing. The saying "Stolen fruit is best" was, I think, most apt in my case. I had never enjoyed anything so much!

We were allowed to wander where we would outside in the surrounding countryside. There was something wonderful everywhere. One day we were running along and I was in front when I saw what I thought was a lovely smooth stretch of grass; I raced on to it and great was my surprise to find myself sinking into what seemed to me to be a large lake, but you couldn't see the water for greenery. This frightened my sister and I very much. I scrambled out soaking wet and raced back to the cottage very upset, only to be told to be more careful. I had fallen into a watercress bed.

To start with we had great battles with the local children, whom we called Country Bumpkins while they called us City Slickers. But on the whole they were a friendly lot and once we really became acquainted we were all great friends. On going exploring one day, my sister and I climbed a hill and found ourselves on some rough land, which was dotted all over with little bumps which we were very puzzled about. We wondered what could be the cause of them. Now I always had a very vivid imagination and I suddenly felt certain in my mind what they were. They were dogs' graves and this was a dogs' graveyard, so we must tread carefully round the graves. And for the rest of the holiday we picked wild flowers and went each day to put them on as many dogs' graves as we could. (I have since found out that they were molehills.)

I do not think the sun stopped shining all that lovely fortnight and, as the time came near for us to go home, we heard the news that war had broken out. All the trains were being used for troops. Oh! how we hoped there wouldn't be a train for us. We were told we might have to stay on. But alas we did go home, brown and well.

✳ ✳ ✳ ✳ ✳

CHAPTER TWENTY-NINE

My Mother's Holiday

I WAS GROWING UP and it was the summer holiday in my thirteenth year. I had been taught to clean the house, to make beds, cook and sew and as I was the eldest girl I looked after my youngest brother, Sydney, who was then a very small boy. He was the baby and we all spoiled him. At this time my father decided to take Mother for a week's holiday to Gorleston, which is near Great Yarmouth. He said I was quite able to keep house and look after Sydney while they were away. I was very pleased to think I was to be in charge of everything, and made up my mind to do the best I could. And so they went on their holiday.

It seemed a very long time, but the day at last came when they returned. I expected to see my mother looking well and happy but I could see she was not. When the opportunity arose I asked her what was wrong. My mother had a gold watch and chain which had belonged to her mother, and she thought a lot of it. She told me she had had a lovely holiday. Father had been most generous. He had insisted that she be measured for a dress, which she was quite delighted with. He took her to shows and paid the Boarding House bill. She couldn't understand how he had managed to save so much. One day towards the end of the week, she asked him how he had managed it. Feeling in his waistcoat pocket he brought out a pawn ticket and showed it to her. He had pawned her watch and chain to pay for the holiday. My mother was most upset about this, and after that each time she wore the dress he had had made for her she would think about the holiday, which had been quite spoiled. It was many weeks before enough money was saved to redeem the watch and chain from the pawn shop. On thinking about it now, I expect my father would not have told Mother if she had not asked about it. I think he expected to redeem the watch and chain and then she would not have known how he had obtained the money. He must have wanted to take her away and this was the only means of doing so.

CHAPTER THIRTY

The First World War

DURING the First World War food was very hard to get and we went short of many things. Father applied for a job which was advertised. He was granted an interview and told to sign a form. This he did, thinking it would secure him a new job. Great was his surprise when he was handed a shilling and told he was now in the Army. It appeared that each new recruit was handed the King's shilling on joining the Army. He came home most upset for he had never been away from home before.

He was sent to Sandwich, in Kent, and was in the cookhouse there for the four years of the war. Robert also joined up and was sent to France, so only my mother and we four children were left.

There were no ration books and no organised rationing. You just got what you could. We would queue up for an hour for a pound of potatoes, seed potatoes so small they had to be cooked in their jackets. There was no butter or meat for us but sometimes we would get $\frac{1}{2}$ lb. of margarine, which Mother would melt and to which she would then add a meat cube in an attempt to give it a little flavour.

One year at Christmas, there being nothing else to eat, Mother made a large plain boiled pudding which she served to us with some golden syrup (saved for an emergency). I thought it quite funny to be having such a dinner on Christmas Day, but Mother sat and cried as she watched us eat it. We lived on meatless stews, which somehow she made quite tasty.

We had many air raids but there was no damage near to us. On top of the warehouse next to the tenements, there was a searchlight operated by a local man affectionately known as Searchlight Charlie. If he switched the searchlight on we knew there would be a raid. Then we would quickly run down to the Shoreway opposite and look to see if the arms of Tower Bridge were up. If they were, this really confirmed that a raid was expected. Most people would go into the vaults of the wharves for safety, but my mother would not go. She preferred to stay indoors. She would push the table against the wall and we would sit on the floor underneath it until the "All Clear" sounded.

There was a great hatred for the Germans during this time and many innocent people of German extraction who lived in our community were treated very cruelly. For instance the local baker and his family (of whom I have already told you something). We were all very friendly before the war came, but then they were suddenly looked upon as enemies. Former customers stoned their shop windows and raided their home. I do not know where they went, but life was made so unbearable for them that they left the district.

Those were sad days, for many men went from our little community and so few returned. We were lucky, for after the war my father returned and my brother came home. He obviously had a bad time in France, but he would not discuss it. He said that he just wanted to forget. This was to have been "The War to End All Wars". Little did we know what the next one was to bring . . . but that is another story.

✳ ✳ ✳ ✳ ✳

CHAPTER THIRTY-ONE

Religious Mania

AFTER THE WAR my father somehow managed to get back into his old job. He was made charge hand and had a few men under him. The wharf where he worked housed many goods, potatoes, tinned fruit, salmon, eggs and rubber goods including boots and plimsolls. These were but a few of the many things stored there.

About this time we were still attending Sunday School each week and the services there were making a great impression on me. I think it was at this Sunday School that I decided I would live a Christian life. It seemed to me that if I could do this all my troubles would be over, for would not God help me in my daily life as my Sunday School teacher had said?

I do not know why he began to pilfer but my father started bringing home little things which at first I took no notice of: a few potatoes, a tin of salmon or a tin of fruit. But after a time I began to be most concerned in case he was caught. One day I told him how worried I was. He assured me that they were from spare cases which nobody had claimed and that I was not to worry. He said "If I do not have them they will be swept into the river. What is better, to take them or see them wasted?" This satisfied me for a while, but I knew it was stealing. Gradually it happened on a bigger scale. I would try to hide the things he brought home, fearing the police might come one day and search the place. I was frightened but I could not tell anyone for fear of giving my father away.

On Sundays a tin of salmon or fruit would be opened and everyone would enjoy it except me. Then I had an idea. I would refuse to eat anything he brought home. Perhaps if I showed him I was a Christian and stood against what he was doing this might stop him. And so one Sunday at tea-time as he handed the salmon round and asked for my plate I said, "I do not want any."

He wanted to know why and so I told him I could not eat what I knew was stolen. To my surprise he started crying, saying that he had not thought his daughter would turn on him as I was doing. I felt miserable and in the evening he had a talk with me. He told me that I had religious mania, and that he would have to have me put away if I continued to act in this way. As I did not want to be put away I consented to eat what he brought home, but I felt I had failed as a Christian. This state of affairs lasted until my mother died. I do not know if it continued after my father remarried but I very much doubt it.

CHAPTER THIRTY-TWO

Tragedies

THERE WERE many tragedies in our little community and as each one happened we would all sorrow with the family concerned.

The tenements were six stories high and people who lived on the top floor had to climb six flights of stone steps and walk along six stone passages to reach their homes. Two front doors gave on to each passage, and behind each front door lived a family. A low brick balcony ran along the end of each passage, letting a little daylight into the windows of the flats. These balconies were not guarded and it was quite possible for us children to climb up on to them and look over to the street below. On one occasion a little boy of about five years overbalanced and was impaled on the railings below. On another occasion a little friend of ours fell from a similar balcony, which was at the back of each flat, and he fell into the yard. Both children were killed, yet nothing was done to prevent such accidents happening. Nobody seemed to care, except the sorrowing parents and we neighbours.

Many children were drowned as the result of going down to the Shoreways for a paddle or swim. Some were sucked under moored barges. I do not want to depress you with these stories which I do assure you are perfectly true. I merely wish to let you know how lucky you are, for in this day and age, children have the first priority.

Many new-born babies were suffocated while lying in bed with their parents. Because not many babies had cots they mostly slept in their parents' bed; mainly I believe to be kept warm, plus the fact that there was no room for a cot even if you could afford one. Some small babies were laid for the first few weeks in a drawer into which their small bodies just fitted.

Then there was the added danger from the horses and carts. It was the practice of every child to run behind the carts and to hang on to the tailboard and slide along (this was one of the ways I wore my boots out so quickly!). It was great fun, but sometimes if you were seen by the driver he would fling his long whip behind to shake you off. Many times a child would be trodden under a horse's hooves as in his efforts to avoid the whip he would run off, only to be knocked down by the horse drawing the cart behind. In vain were we warned of these dangers, but I'm sorry to say that we knew no fear and continued as before.

CHAPTER THIRTY-THREE

Epidemics

EVERY YEAR about September we would have an epidemic. It seemed to go in cycles. One year it would be Scarlet Fever, another year Diphtheria and in my early years it was sometimes Smallpox. Of course, Tuberculosis was with us all the time. I think that most of the infectious diseases were brought about by the conditions we lived in.

In the tenements six families used one drainpipe leading to one sink for their waste water. The smells which came from these sinks are indescribable. They were never cleaned and must have been the breeding ground for all kinds of germs. Then there were the rats, which in some cases were nearly as big as cats. And everyone's house was infested with bed bugs, which were most horrible. You would wake up in the morning to find you had been bitten in many places. These bites were very uncomfortable and embarrassing, because everyone knew what they were. My sister and I would rub ourselves with vinegar before we went to bed hoping the bugs would not come near us but alas! they came just the same. Nothing seemed to stop them. I remember my father going round each window frame and doorpost with a blowlamp, burning the bugs which lined the crevices. Mother would go round the beds and mattresses with white vinegar which could burn your hands if you happened to spill a drop on them. But these bugs must have been Cockney bugs. They were tough and nothing could stop them breeding.

One year, during a Scarlet Fever epidemic, we five children caught it and all of us were taken to isolation hospitals in different parts of London. I was taken by ambulance through the streets, and across Tower Bridge to the south side of the river. There, near the Surrey Commercial Docks, I was taken by stretcher on to a pier and from there carried aboard an isolation boat, where I spent the night in a bunk. In the morning I was taken down river to Dartford Isolation Pier and from here to Joyce Green Hospital at Dartford. It was quite an experience but I felt too ill to enjoy it. I can still remember the name of that boat: it was the "Maltese Cross". These isolation boats were paddle steamers, kept for the express purpose of transferring infectious people to hospital.

Diphtheria was a deadly disease and if it was not treated in time could kill in a few hours. If one member of the family caught it, in most cases everyone else in that family caught it too. In the case both of Scarlet

Fever and of Diphtheria the Sanitary Inspector had to be notified. He would send men along with a van, into which they put the mattress and bedding to take them away for fumigating. Then they lit sulphur candles in the infected bedroom, and sealed the door and windows with sticky tape. The room had to be left unopened for forty-eight hours. You might have thought this process would have killed the bugs too, but after the beds were returned, back they came! People fought a losing battle, for the bugs always won.

If you walked the length of the High Street you came to the gasworks. Mothers of little children who had Whooping Cough would take them to walk about in the close vicinity of the gasworks in the hope of making them sick. It was generally believed that this was good for the child. The smell from the gasworks was most unpleasant and fumy and certainly could in some cases make the child sick. The mothers, in their ignorance, did not mind where the child was sick, as long as it *was* sick, and believed that being sick relieved the congestion on the chest. Once having achieved their aim, they took their poor mite home, only to repeat the treatment until the child eventually lost the cough. In some cases this went on for weeks, and many children were cross-eyed after a bad attack of Whooping Cough. Luckily the children of today have injections before this distressing complaint has a chance to take hold.

Only those who witnessed these unnecessary things can truly be thankful that such things do not happen today.

CHAPTER THIRTY-FOUR

Ignorance

THE DEATH RATE among small babies was very high. As I mentioned, many babies were suffocated in bed. Others were lain on by cats. These cats would seemingly watch for a chance to lie across a baby's face and in a very short time the child would be dead.

When a new baby arrived we would hear people ask "has it come to stay?" If it lived for a month then you were sure that you were going to rear it. Many of the babies were poor sickly things, with a great dummy always stuck in their mouths. If the dummy fell on to the ground it was picked up and cleaned in the mouth of whoever was nearest before being popped back into the baby's mouth again.

Rickets! You should have seen the poor little legs, bandy and bent, too frail to take the weight of the tiny bodies. Mothers would breast-feed their babies until they were two years old in the hope of keeping themselves from having another baby, for it was a common belief that they couldn't conceive while breast feeding. (As far as I know there were no contraceptives at that time.) I do not think people knew how to prevent more babies arriving. This subject was never spoken of in my young days, it was considered a dirty subject and one to be avoided. Many young girls had babies. Certainly most of them were ignorant of the facts of life. I myself was never told anything about babies and when my first child was about to be born I was most shocked to find out how she would arrive. I had imagined my tummy would open to let the baby out. With such widespread ignorance it is small wonder that so many babies died soon after birth.

When a baby was born it was dressed in a fashion very different to that of today. Babies were generally supposed to have weak backs and so a stiff binder about six inches wide was wound about their middle. The binder went round many times so that when it was fastened the child was well and truly encased by it. Then came a long flannel petti-coat. This was turned up at the bottom and fastened with two safety pins. It looked like an envelope with its flap turned up and it prevented the child from kicking or moving its legs. Over this went the long night-dress. Plastic pants had not been invented so the child was almost always soaking wet and smelly.

These long clothes were worn until the baby was six weeks or two months old, according to its size and progress. Then they were "short-ened". Both boys and girls were then put in frocks and petticoats. Boys stayed in these until they were two years old. Then off came the petticoat and dress, and knickers took their place. This was called "being breeched".

A new baby would always have a veil over its face. What this was for I do not know, unless it was to keep the flies away. We were pestered by flies in summer. People would buy fly-papers and hang them up to trap the flies on. These were long pieces of sticky paper. You saw them every-where in homes and shops.

If a baby was troublesome, its mother made sugar-teats for it to suck. A small piece of bread was soaked in water and shaped into a ball about the size of a marble. It was coated with a little sugar, put in a piece of rag and tied with a length of cotton. About a dozen would be made at a time and placed on a saucer. If the baby started to cry one was popped into its mouth. I'm glad to say this practice has now stopped. It was so easy for a baby to swallow one of these sugar-teats.

Funerals were a common sight in Wapping. They were always very grand affairs, for no matter how poor a family might be it always gave its members a good funeral. The body was kept at home for a week after the death and put on show for people to see. It had to be displayed for a full week in case people thought you were hurrying the body away. Funerals were horse-drawn. The animals would be glossy and black with long black plumes on their heads and velvet palls hanging on either side of them. The top of the hearse was completely covered with plumes and was attended by bearers in long black coats and tall crepe-covered hats. People from throughout the district would gather outside the house of the dead man and line up on either side on the pavement to give him a good send-off. After the funeral was over and the mourners had returned, a good meal was provided for them by sympathetic neighbours and friends. After the funeral, the family wore black as a sign of mourning, and this was not discarded until a year had passed.

In the case of a very small baby where the family had no money, for a small consideration the undertaker would place the baby in with an adult corpse. Nobody in the dead man's family was any the wiser.

CHAPTER THIRTY-FIVE

Leaving School

I WAS NOW nearing school-leaving age and as I had not the least idea of what I wanted to do my father decided that I was to go into service. But this I would *not* do. I wanted to stay at home, where my mother was.

I think my whole life centred around my mother, partly I suppose because she was never well and she relied on me taking her place when she had to stay in bed, and partly because I had a fear of the world outside our community. And so, with it settled that I was not going into service, I left school at the age of fourteen and began the hunt for a job. I was very small for fourteen, with two long plaits of hair which reached to my waist. When young ladies left school they were expected to put their hair up and let their dresses down, just to show that they were now grown up. One morning Mother went with me to Aldgate, where we had heard a girl was wanted. It was at an Express Dairy Restaurant and they wanted a "runner", someone who ran about for the waitresses and at the same time learnt to wait at tables. We met the supervisor who, as soon as she saw me, asked my mother if she was sure I really was fourteen, for I was so small. When she was shown my Birth Certificate she was satisfied as to my age and said I could have the job on condition that I put my hair up. The wages were 6s. per week, less 1s. 6d. for dinners, leaving 4s. 6d. to take home. Out of this my father gave me 6d. for my pocket-money. The remaining 4s. went towards my keep.

The first day at the restaurant was a nightmare. I had to wear a black dress, and a white apron and cap. I tried to put my hair up but it kept on falling down because it was so heavy. The other girls there were much older than I was and were very kind to me. After a little while I was sent to wait on a lady. On reaching the table I recognised the customer as our own District Nurse, a very severe person whom we all feared. I was just as scared of her as anyone else was. I timidly went and stood to take her order. At that moment my hair fell down again. She took not a scrap of notice and gave me her order as if she had not seen me. After that embarrassing episode, one of the other girls suggested that I plait my hair and fasten the plaits along the top of my head. With the aid of a whole packet of hairpins I managed to do this. I continued at that restaurant for a long time and learnt to be a very good waitress.

But at home things were not so good. Mother now rarely left her bed and so it was decided that I should give up going to work and stay at home to look after her and the rest of the family. She had been attending Guy's Hospital and the specialists there decided she should be admitted for an operation to remove a second tumour. She came through the operation well and was home after three weeks. I had to go to Guy's once a fortnight for her medicine, and when she was able she would go to see the doctor.

I always accompanied her on these visits. One day the doctor called me in, leaving my mother to dress in another room. He spoke very kindly to me and asked if I had a father. I replied that I had. Then he said "Go home and tell him that your mother has cancer and cannot live longer than six months." I could not do what he told me. I just could not bring myself to tell my father . . . and so I told no-one. I could hardly believe it myself. What should I do? It was just not possible for this to happen. I spent many sleepless nights and would creep into her bedroom in the early morning and watch to see if she was still breathing.

After a fortnight I went back to the hospital and saw the doctor. I confessed to him that I had not told my father that Mother was soon to die. He said that Father must know and I was to ask him to come to the hospital, where he would talk to him. Father duly went. When he came home I asked him if he knew. His reply was "I don't believe it, and neither must you." But I did believe it.

And so began long months of anguish and worry. I told Kathleen, and that helped quite a lot. She had now left school and we were very good friends, going around and doing everything together. About this time we joined the Girls Guild which met in the Old Mahogany Bar. This was a branch of the Wesleyan East End Mission and was situated about half-an-hour's walk from home. Our meeting was held once a week, on Tuesday evenings at 7.30. We did Swedish drill, country dancing, played badminton and formed a choir. This one evening we enjoyed very much. Mixing with other girls of our own age we soon made many friends. Tuesday was the one evening which I looked forward to all week.

I had now taken my mother's place in the home and did the weekly wash, cooked, shopped and looked after my father, my sister and brothers. In return my father gave me 1s. 6d. a week for pocket money, which even in those far-off days was very little. The girls at the Guild would arrange little outings in the summer from which I would nearly always excuse myself, having, of course, no money with which to pay my share. My sister would go and I felt very bitter when she went and I did not. Kathleen was now out at work and earned a fair wage. She paid £1 a week towards her keep, and could afford to buy herself nice clothes. The fact that I was still dependent on Father for mine led to some grumbling on my part, but he said I was quite well off, having 1s. 6d. and my food and shelter. However, Kathleen started giving me 1s. a week out of her wages, bringing my weekly pocket-money up to 2s. 6d.

Mother was confined to bed almost all the time, and so life for me was pretty full. I had now got used to the thought that one day we should be without her, but the worry was always there. The medicine from the hospital which I collected once a fortnight contained opium and had the effect of making her so drowsy that she was always half asleep. And when she was awake she did not know much of what went on around her. My father now realised the truth of the situation and sat with her each evening until bedtime, feeling, I think, as helpless as I did. We did not speak about it, but just waited. Time went on and still she lived.

* * * * *

CHAPTER THIRTY-SIX

The Locked Model

I FOUND IT a hard struggle to make the housekeeping money last from one week to another. Father only gave me £1 10s. a week, saying I must learn to be thrifty, and from the housekeeping money I had to pay the rent, which was 7s. 6d. a week. I also managed to put a little away for insurance. But at least Father always paid for the coal, and we were never without a good fire.

As far as I can remember, my weekly housekeeping budget looked something like the list shown on the opposite page.

The "special haddock" had to be bought from a shop in Aldgate called Gowers, half-an-hour's walk away. It was cut in two, half each for Mother and Father. We children took it in turns to have the ears. Our bread was dipped in the water in which it had been cooked. We thought it tasted very nice.

There must have been other items which I have now forgotten, but you can see that after I had done the weekend shopping there was, very little left with which to manage the rest of the week. I would tell my father I had no money left and he would give me some, saying he would have to stop it from the next week's housekeeping. He kept his word, with the result that I was always short, and could never start with a full week's money. I tried desperately to economise but could never make the money last.

	£	s.	d.
Rent		7	6
14 loaves @ 2½d. per loaf (2 lbs)		2	11
2 lb. margarine @ 4½d. per lb.			9
2 tins condensed milk @ 4½d. per tin			9
12 lbs potatoes @ ½d. per lb.			6
Meat for week		3	0
4 lbs sugar (yellow crystals) @ 2d. per lb.			8
½ lb. tea @ 1s. 4d. per lb.			8
Sundries		1	0
Fish (i.e. 1 special haddock for Father and Mother)		1	2
Fish—herrings, mackerel or kippers			6
Vegetables—cabbage, pot herbs, beetroots or parsnips			6
Butter—¼ lb. for Mother			4½
1 new-laid egg for Mother			6
1 lb. plum tomatoes (in season)			1
Milk for Mother and milk puddings		1	1
Egg yolk			6
Gas per week		3	6
Insurance		1	4
	£1	7	3½

I recall most vividly one event in particular, which I think must have occurred at about this time for I remember I was already keeping house. Father used to leave his trousers hanging on the brass knob on my mother's bed. One day I took five shillings from his pocket, hoping he would not miss it. But that same evening he asked who had been down his pocket and I had to confess it was I. This five shillings was also stopped from the next week's housekeeping. At this time I believe he was earning quite good money, but he would never spend any.

In my mother's bedroom we had a model of a house. On opening the front door two drawers were exposed. The side doors revealed more drawers. Father always kept this model locked, and this made me wonder what he had in the drawers. One day when he went out, he forgot to take the key with him. Now was my opportunity! I would see what was inside. Carefully I unlocked the doors and pulled open the drawers. To my great surprise I saw them filled with piles of £1 notes, all neatly tied in packets. I could not believe my eyes. Here were *hundreds* of pounds. Yet I could not have a little more for the housekeeping! Looking at this, I realised that my father had become a miser.

I must confess that I took £1 from that pile of money and added it to my housekeeping. The very next day he asked me if I had been to the model as he had left the key by accident. He said he had a little money in it and there was £1 missing. I denied having been there. He believed me, but to this day that £1 note has always been on my conscience.

*****

CHAPTER THIRTY-SEVEN

Unexpected Meeting

ONE DAY while I was slicing some meat in preparation for dinner I cut my thumb rather badly. As it would not stop bleeding I ran to a neighbour's house and asked her to bandage it for me. She was very kind, and willingly cleaned and covered the cut. Then she insisted that I went to hospital. She went with me and stayed while I had it stitched. This episode resulted in us becoming friends, and from that day on she would often invite me in for a cup of tea in the afternoons while Mother was sleeping.

She had a large family of girls and boys, of whom I met all but one. While I was there one day a young man let himself in. I was introduced to him, and learned that he was Reuben, the only one of her sons whom I had not met before. He worked on the river and was seldom home. I was most surprised when he asked me if I would like to go with him to see a show. I had never had a boy-friend and was rather shy of boys. But Reuben seemed quiet and almost as shy as I was. Of course, I had first to ask my father whether I might go. He didn't like the idea but gave me his permission.

76

This was to be the beginning of the courtship with the man who is now my husband. We went about together whenever he was home and I could get away. He asked me to marry him many times but I felt I could not leave my mother now that she was so ill. Three times I gave him up, only to come together with him again. He would say "Why won't you marry me?" and I would reply "How can I leave my mother and father, my brothers and my sister? Who is to look after them if I go?" But he always replied "Once your mother is gone, then what will happen to you?"

CHAPTER THIRTY-EIGHT

The Old Mahogany Bar

MY ELDEST BROTHER, Robert, was now married. I was in my twenties, and Reuben had persuaded me to become engaged to him. Kathleen had promised to stay and look after Mother if I wanted to get married. She was willing to give up her job and take my place, so plans were made for Reuben and I to be married.

I had become so attached to the friends and people of the Old Mahogany Bar that I felt I would like to be married there. I must explain this to you. Before it became a Mission Hall it was known as Wilton's Music Hall. It had been a place of very bad repute, being in the area where many sailors stayed while their ships were in dock. It was a place to which women would lure them. When they had plied them with drink they robbed them of all their wages. The sailors were then dropped through a trap-door and carried, unconscious, along underground passages which lead out into some back streets in Stepney's Highway. When they regained consciousness they of course had no idea how they came to be there. Wilton's Music Hall was eventually closed, and in 1888 it was re-opened as a Mission Hall.

It was situated in an alley called Graces Alley, in the middle of a very rough area. Put to its new use it was a happy place, full of young people who really enjoyed the many amenities offered them. For the boys there was bagatelle, a gymnasium and a band; and for the girls netball, badminton, a choir and a girls' Life Brigade. What happy times we had there! It was one of the very few places in those drab surroundings where happiness could be found. On Sundays there were services which were so bright, with singing so wonderful that you felt you must go. We went because we wanted to. No-one attended against their will. We all dearly loved our Pastor, who was a real friend to all of us. He would often come to visit my mother, and when he knew I wanted to be married at the "Bar", he arranged for it to be licensed for marriages just for us.

And so, on a day in July we were at last married. My mother got up and was taken to the wedding. But she did not go out again. She died six weeks afterwards.

✻ ✻ ✻ ✻ ✻

CHAPTER THIRTY-NINE

The Old Home Again

I HAVE mentioned the Salvationist who used to visit us (the lady with whom I went to see the old barrel-organist and his wife). She was the only person my father welcomed to our home. She was about forty years old and we all liked her very much. She had regularly visited my mother once a week. If Father happened to be in we would all notice his face light up as soon as he saw her. Mother had seen this too and had remarked "There is your next wife". How true her words were to prove, for, within three months of Mother's death, the Salvationist became Father's second wife. But she was not as my mother had been, who always submitted to my father's will. Now it was Father's turn to give in to his wife's wishes. She would not live in the tenements and so a house was found in Clapton, where they lived until my father died.

Reuben and I had found two rooms in a Jewish house in Whitechapel, for which we paid £5 key money and a rent of 14s. a week. I was not happy there, so when Father decided to leave our old home I applied for the tenancy, and got it. So I really began my married life in the same place as I had spent my childhood.

By the time my father had been remarried for a few weeks Reuben and I had painted and cleaned the old flat and rid it of its vermin. How pretty it looked, with its gay curtains and new lino! We forgot the ugliness of

the outside world and rejoiced in the home we had now made together. My mother seemed to be there too, and I felt that she rejoiced with us.

One evening as we were preparing supper, there came a knock at the door. I opened it and there stood Kathleen, weeping. She explained that things were not going smoothly between her and my father's new wife. She begged to be allowed to live with us. Later that evening Father came and asked if she would return with him, but she would not go. So he went back, leaving my sister to live with us. We were very happy to have her for, as I have told you, we were always great friends.

After a day or two my brother William came, saying that he also wanted to be with me. Now here was a problem. How could I put a grown girl and boy in the one spare room we had? There was nothing for it but to do what my mother had done before me: divide the room in two with a large curtain.

And so we were a family again but for Sydney, my youngest brother, who was only fourteen years old and had to stay with Father. As the years went by he was my father's only friend and comforter. For Father once confided in me that he had made a mistake in his second marriage. I think he regretted it to the end of his life.

✳ ✳ ✳ ✳ ✳

CHAPTER FORTY

The Perfect Baby

WE HAD BEEN MARRIED a few months and I knew my first baby was coming. How we planned and hoped. My sister and I knitted and sewed. Never was a baby wanted so much. We all hoped for a girl, but I do not think we would have minded what it was, so great was our joy at its coming.

Reuben returned from work one day with a friend who worked with him on the river. He was a young man who had recently lost his wife in childbirth, leaving him with a little two-year-old son to look after. He met Kathleen and they fell in love. In a short time they were married. So my sister started her married life with a ready-made baby. I'm glad to say it has been a very happy marriage. She has had children of her own and the little boy is now a man, with a wife and family of his own. My brother Robert also found a nice girl and married her.

At last Reuben and I were really on our own. Our baby duly arrived, a little girl whom we named Kathleen, after my sister. I thought, as all mothers do, that she was the most perfect baby ever born. How we loved her! And how I loved to show her off. But I did not want her to grow up in those surroundings. I wanted a garden and flowers and trees for her. I began to hate those high brick walls. I wanted to be able to put my baby in a lovely clean place, not as that place was with its noise and dirt.

As I have said, I was a pushing sort of child, and in growing up I had become a fighter. I would fight for what I wanted and keep on fighting until I got it. I had changed from a timid, shy person into a determined one, with but a single thought in my mind. My children were to have a different life from the one I had known.

✳ ✳ ✳ ✳ ✳

CHAPTER FORTY-ONE

I Make a Choice and get a New Home

KATHLEEN was already a few months old, and each day I would try to take her to the little park in which my sister and I had played as children. There she might lie and watch the leaves as the wind rustled them. There we could get away for a little while from the noise of the wharves and the rumble of the traffic.

On returning home one afternoon I found the street door open. On going in I found that the flat had been burgled while we had been out at the park. Things had been thrown from the drawers on to the floor. The wardrobe had been ransacked and Reuben's best suit stolen. The gas meter had been emptied. In fact anything of any value had been taken. We were most upset about this and though we called the Police we did not find the thief.

The burglary made me more determined than ever that we should get away from those surroundings, but we knew of no way of doing so. A few days later I had an idea. I had heard of a new housing estate which was being developed at Dagenham, in Essex. The developers were the

London County Council. I decided I would try for one of those houses so one morning I dressed Kathleen in her prettiest outfit and made my way to County Hall, the headquarters of the London County Council, at Westminster.

It was a very long journey but we made it. On reaching the building I wondered what on earth I should say. I half wished I hadn't gone, but there I was and I would try at any rate. I asked to see the Housing Officer. The clerk wanted to know if I had an appointment. I had not thought of this, but I explained that I had come such a long way and I was sure I could see someone. I was told to wait and after a long time the Housing Officer called me into his office. He was quite nice and started to admire the baby. I knew this was my chance and I said "She is lovely, isn't she?" He agreed. "Have you any children?" I asked. "Yes" he said. "Have you a garden for them?" "Yes, I have." "She has no garden. She has nothing! I wonder if you would like to visit the place where I live? Am I asking too much for her? You are building houses. Why can't we have one where we can bring our children up in decent surroundings?" I stopped talking, not quite believing I had said those things, and to an entire stranger. "Go home now" he said. "I'll see what I can do, but this sort of thing is most irregular."

So home I went, feeling that I had wasted my time. However, a few days afterwards a letter came, together with a form to complete. It was an application for a house on the Dagenham Estate. We filled in the form, and waited. After about a month another letter came, which said that a house was waiting for us.

Then a queer feeling came over me. I wanted to go but I wanted to stay. Here was home. Here were friends and neighbours. Here were the people with whom I had grown up. Suddenly it all became very dear to me. I hated it but now I didn't want to leave it. But I looked at my baby and I knew I must go, for her sake and for others which might follow her.

And so we moved to the new house, leaving behind for ever the old life between high walls.

Epilogue

Oh, high brick walls a-standing
So grim and stark and bare
On dirty grimy roadways
You have no beauty there.
Wharves, docks and ships surround you,
All is noise and din.
Can you not see the little child
You mercilessly close in.

Can you not see she hungers
For grass and flowers or trees,
Clean fields on which to play in,
Blue skies above to see.

Oh, high brick walls take warning:
She will not always stay
Beneath your dark and gloomy shade—
Like me, she'll run away.

W. W. Jameson

BOROUGH ENGINEER.

JUNE 1902.